Economic Concepts Ancient and Modern

Ratan Lal Basu

Economic Concepts Ancient and Modern

Ratan Lal Basu

Published by Kautilya, 2023.

Economic Concepts Ancient and Modern

ECONOMIC CONCEPTS ANCIENT AND MODERN

First edition. January 30, 2023.

ISBN: 979-8215513637

Written by Ratan Lal Basu.

Economic Concepts Ancient and Modern

Contents

Chapter 1. Environment and Ecology in Arthaśāstra

Introduction

Recent awareness and in many cases fuss about environment and ecology arose only since the middle of the twentieth century. In fact, the current wave of environment awareness got a fillip only after the "United Nations Conference on Human Environment" held in 1972 at Stockholm (Sweden), and the matter gained further importance after the "Earth Summit" held in 1992 at Rio de Janeiro (Brazil). However during the early 20th century Rabindranath Tagore dealt in detail with various aspects of environment (and in a more coherent way than the present day piece meal analysis) in various writings.[1] In this regard he derived inspiration from ancient Indian texts. Vedic Samhitās, Upanishadas, Purānas, the Rāmāyana, the Mahābhārata, Dharmaśāstras, Arthaśāstras etc. embodied rules and regulations relevant to preservation of environment and ecology. Unlike the present day piecemeal and *ad hoc* approach towards the issue ancient Indian environment consciousness was holistic in its approach and it sprang from the Upanishadic gospel 'Vasudhaiva kūtumbakam', i.e., all the beings of the entire universe belong to the same family. Among the ancient Indian texts, Kautilya's Arthaśāstra is most secular and pragmatic in its approach as it was designed to specify rules which could be enforced by law by the king. In this article we are going to take up some important prescriptions embodied in the Arthasastra for preservation of environment and ecology.

Prevention of Man-made Hazards

Kautilya entrusted the task of protecting forests and other natural resources with the king [through different state officials]. He prescribed that appropriate plants should be grown to protect dry lands and pasturelands should be properly protected. The king should protect different types of forests, water reservoirs and mines. To quote:

II/1/39: Thus the king should protect the product-forests, elephant-forests, irrigation works and mines that were made in ancient times and should start new ones.

II/2/4: And he should established on its border or in conformity with the (suitability of the) land, another animal park where all animals are (welcomed) as guests (and given full protection).

II/2/5: And he should establish forests, one each for the products indicated as forest produce ....

II/2/6: On the border (of the kingdom), he should establish a forest for elephants guarded by foresters.

II/2/7: The superintendent of the elephant-forest should, with the help of guards of the elephant-forest, protect the elephant-forest (whether) on the mountain, along a river, along lakes or in marshy tracts, with its boundaries, entrances and exits (fully) known.

II/2/8: They should kill anyone slaying an elephant.

Houses and other dwelling places, roads, cremation grounds etc. should be properly constructed preserving environment. Every house should have proper arrangements for controlling fire. Any violation of the rules pertaining to these matters would make one liable to punishment. To quote:

II/4/1: Three royal highways running west to east and three running south to north, that should be the division of the residential area.

Every house should be constructed strictly on the basis of the rules [preserving environment] prescribed by the authorities. There should be proper arrangements in each house for sewage and proper disposal of wastes. The violators would be fined according to the gravity of the offence.

III/8/6: (He should make) the dung-hill, the water-course or the well, not in a place other than that suited to the house, except the water-ditch for a woman in confinement till the end of ten days (from delivery).

III/8/7: In case of transgression of that, the lowest fine for violence (shall be imposed).

III/8/9: He should cause to be made a deep-flowing water-course or one falling in a cascade, three *padas* away (from a neighbour's wall) or one *aratni* and a half (away).

III/8/10: In case of transgression of that, the fine is fifty-four *panas*.

III/8/11: He should cause to be made a place for carts and quadrupeds, a fire-place, a place for the large water-jar, the grinding mill or the pounding machine, one *pada* away or one *aratni* (from a neighbour's wall).

III/8/12: In case of transgression of that, the fine is twenty-four *panas*.

III/8/13: Between all two structures or two projecting rooms, (there is to be) an open lane one *kishku* (wide) or three *padas*.

III/8/14: Between them, the distance between the eaves of roofs (is to be) four *aňgulas*, or one may over-lay the other.

III/8/15: He should cause to be made a side-door in the intervening lane, measuring one *kisku*, for making repairs to what is damaged, not (allowing) crowding.

III/8/16: For light, he should cause a small window to be made high up.

III/8/19: And he should cause that part above the verandah which requires protection, to be covered by matting, or a wall touching (the roof), for fear of damage by rain.

In the above specifications Kautilya takes into consideration all aspects necessary for perfect harmony in dwelling places of the citizens.

Kautilya prescribes various fines and� other punitive measures for polluting the environment by throwing dirt on the roads and highways or voiding urine and faeces at public places.

II/36/26: For throwing dirt on the road the fine shall be one eight (of a *pana*), for blocking it with muddy water, one quarter.

II/36/27: On the royal highway, (the fines shall be) double.

II/36/28: Fines for voiding faeces in a holy place, in a place for water, in a temple and in royal property are one *pana* rising successively by one *pana*, half these for passing urine.

But Kautilya was wise enough to realize that sometimes people are compelled to commit the above mischief due to illness or similar reason. In that case the miscreant is exempted from fines. To quote:

II/36/29: If (these are) due to medicine, illness or fear, (the persons are) not to be fined.

Throwing carcasses or dead bodies at public places in the city are punishable by fines. To quote:

II/36/30: For throwing the dead body of a cat, a dog, a ichneumon or a serpent inside the city, the fine shall be three *panas*; for throwing the dead body a donkey, a camel, a mule, a horse or cattle, six *panas*; for a human corpse, fifty *panas*.

The dead bodies are to be cremated at cremation grounds only. Otherwise the offender will have to pay fines. To quote:

II/36/33: For depositing burning (a corpse) elsewhere than in a cremation ground, the fine (shall be) twelve *panas*.

Kautilya also prescribes that every one should be careful about preserving common property and bio-diversity. Otherwise he would be fined. To quote:

IV/10/4: In case of theft of deer or objects from deer-parks or produce-forests, (there shall be) a fine of one hundred.

IV/10/5: In case of theft of deer or birds (intended) for show or pleasure or in case of killing these, the fine shall be double.

No one should do anything to have harmful external effects on cultivation, irrigation system and other properties of other persons. Violators of this rule would be punished with fines. In case of setting fire to properties of others or common property, or bursting a dam containing water the punishment is death-sentence. To quote:

III/9/27: In the case of damage to the ploughing or seeds in another's field by the use of a reservoir, channels or a field under water, they shall pay compensation in accordance with the damage.

III/9/28: In case of mutual damage to fields under water, parks and embankments, the fine (shall be) double the damage.

III/9/29: A tank on a lower level, constructed afterwards, shall not flood with water a field watered by a tank on a higher level.

III/9/30: A (tank) constructed on a higher level shall not prevent the flooding with water of a lower tank, except when its use has ceased for three years.

III/9/31: For transgression of that, (the punishment shall be) the lowest fine for violence and the emptying of the tank.

III/10/5: For encroaching on a path for small animals or men the fine is twelve *panas*; on a path for large animals twenty-four *panas*, on a road for elephants or fields fifty-four *panas*, on a road to a dike or a forest one hundred and six, on a road to a cremation ground or a village two hundred, on a road in a *dronamukha* five hundred, on a road in a *sthānīya*, the countryside or pasture land, one thousand.

III/10/6: In case of reducing the size of these (roads), the fines are one-quarter of the fines (mentioned).

III/10/7: In case of ploughing on (them, the fines are) as prescribed.

IV/11/17: For one breaking a dam holding water, drowning in water at the same spot (shall be the punishment), the highest fine for violence if it was without water, the middle if it was in ruins and abandoned.

IV/11/20: He shall cause to be burnt in fire one who sets on fire a pasture, a field, a threshing ground, a house, a produce-forest or an elephant forest.

Prevention of Natural Hazards

Damage to environment may be caused also by natural hazards. All of them cannot be prevented by human material endeavors. But we may prevent some of them by our knowledge of science and coherent �efforts. Kautilya's prescription for disaster management is worth noting, particularly the anticipation of disasters and prior preparation for preventing them as far as possible. First he classifies the disasters caused by nature. To quote:

IV/3/1: There are eight great calamities of a divine origin: fire, floods, disease, famine, rats, wild animals, serpents and evil spirits.

IV/3/2: From them he should protect the country.

Some of the important measures as prescribed by Kautilya to prevent natural hazards are discussed below.

Fire Hazards

The responsibility, of controlling hazards from fire and devising rules for the citizens so as to minimize hazards from fire, lies with the City Superintendent. To quote:

IV/3/4: Prevention of fire is explained in 'Rules for the City Superintendent' and in connection with royal possessions in 'Rules for the Royal Residence'.

Remedies against fire in residential areas and punitive measures against violators of fire-prevention rules are prescribed in the following *ślokas*.

II/36/15: And (citizens shall take) steps against (an outbreak of) fire in summer.

II/36/16: In the two middle quarters of the day, one-eighth (of a *pana*) is the fine for (kindling) fire.

II/36/17: Or they should do their cooking outside (the house).

II/36/18: One quarter (of a *pana* is the fine) for not providing five jars, also a big jar, a trough, a ladder, an axe, a winnowing-basket, a hook, a 'hair-seizer' and a skin-bag.

II/36/23: For the owner, not running to save the house on fire, the fine (shall be) twelve *panas*, six *panas* for a tenant.

II/36/24: In case of (houses) catching fire through negligence, the fine (shall be) fifty-four *panas*.

The role of the City Superintendent as regards fire prevention is described in the following *ślokas*.

II/36/19: The (City-superintendent) should remove things covered with grass or matting.

II/36/20: He shall make those who live by (the use of) fire reside in one locality.

II/36/22: Collections of water-jars should be placed in thousands on roads and at cross-roads, gates and in royal precincts.

Flood Hazards

In the following *ślokas,* Kautilya prescribes measures for prevention of hazards from flood-situations.

IV/3/6: In the rainy season, villages situated near water should live away from the level of the floods.

IV/3/7: And they should keep a collection of wooden planks, bamboos and boats.

Kautilya also emphasizes on mass-participation in rescue works. This is done both by moral suasion and legal measures. To quote:

IV/3/8: They should rescue a (person) being carried away (by the flood) by means of gourds, skin-bags, canoes, tree-stems and rope-braids.

IV/3/9: For those who do not go to the rescue, the fine is twelve *panas*, except in the case of those without canoes.

Famine Hazards

The role of the state in famine management, as prescribed by Kautilya, is noteworthy. The ruler should have prior preparation for anticipated famines so that he is not caught napping. When the disaster actually occurs, he should take quick measures so as to minimize the harmful effects on the masses. The most interesting aspect in these prescriptions is that the ruler should relinquish if he fails to handle the famine situation.

To quote:

IV/3/17: During a famine, the king should make a store of seeds and food-stuffs and show favour (to the subjects), or (institute) the building of forts or water-works with the grant of food, or share (his) provisions (with them), or entrust the country (to another king).

Help of friendly foreign governments may also be sought if it is not possible to manage disaster by the efforts of the government of the affected country alone. To quote:

IV/3/18: Or, he should seek shelter with allies, or cause a reduction or shifting (of the population).

In fact ecological and environmental awareness of Kautilya can be found in almost all the chapters. It is clear from the above discussion that Kautilya was much concerned about matters pertaining to the preservation of environment and ecology. To this end he prescribed various rules and also the punitive measures for violation of such rules. In this regard Kautilya's approach was holistic as he considered preservation of environment and ecology as integral parts of human living.

Relevance for Modern Times

As a follow up of the Stockholm International Conference on Environment in 1972 (mentioned at the beginning of this chapter), several international agencies were formed for the protection of environment and ecology of Earth. Mention-worthy among them are:

1. Convention on International Trade in Endangered Species (CITES)

2. Environmental Protection Agency (EPA)

3. United Nations Environment Program (UNEP)

4. South Asia Co-operative Environment Program (SACEP)

This wave of environment awareness also encouraged the Government of India to pass various Acts to protect environment and ecology. Noted among these Acts are:

1. Water (Prevention and control of pollution) Act, 1974

2. Air (Prevention and control of pollution) Act, 1981
3. Environment (Protection) Act, 1986
4. Motor Vehicles Act, 1998

For implementation of the provisions of these Acts, "The Central Pollution Control Board" at the central level and "State Pollution Control Boards" at the state levels were formed in 1988. "The Department of Environment, Forest and Wild Life" was established

in 1985. Mention worthy among the various Government Agencies, and NGOs [Non-Government Organizations] concerning environment protection in India are:

1. Botanical Survey of India
2. Zoological Survey of India
3. National Wasteland Development Board
4. Central Ganga Authority
5. Bombay Natural History Society
6. Central Forestry Commission
7. Department of Non-conventional Energy Sources
8. Tata Energy Research Institute" (Santra (ed.) 2001)

One major shortcoming of all these measures [both at the national and at the international level] is that they are mainly *ad hoc* in nature and lack holistic approach. In fact, these measures are designed to solve specific problems and do not spring from any basic cosmological and holistic view. So, it has become difficult to coordinate and harmonize various types of activities and agencies designed to protect environment and ecology. These approaches may solve some specific problems pertaining to environment and ecology but would fail to remove the basic cause [which lies in our world outlook and view regarding nature and our relationship with it], which lead to the generation of damage to environment and ecology. In this regard we may learn from the ancient Indian texts like Kautilya's Arthasastra. We are to consider ourselves as a part of the harmonious universe and therefore regulate our material activities in accordance of the rules of nature. This approach towards environment and ecology is likely to generate deeper awareness about these matters among the common people so that they will be more willing to spontaneously co-operate in eco-preserving drives of the government or the NGOs. Kautilya's detailed specifications points out how every measure towards preservation of ecology and environment are coherently integrated.

It is true that environmental and ecological problems are now more severe and complicated than those at the time of Kautilya. Many aspects of environmental problems were totally absent in those days. But if we look deeply into the matter we will realize that all man-made environmental and ecological problems arise because of our greed or ignorance that make us commit things contrary to the balance of nature. The root cause ecological problems is this and therefore same for all ages.

In Kautilya's age, moral preaching were not enough to prevent people from committing eco-damaging activities. So, he specifies punitive measures by the state for violating rules intended to maintain environment and ecology. All these approaches differ from the present ad hoc approach in the sense that we today do not go into the essence of the matter, and we treat every problem in isolation but not as the integral part of our living. Another important aspect of Kautilya's prescriptions is that he considers rescue of people from disasters a moral obligation of the ruler and he has no moral right to continue ruling if he fails to manage the disasters in �the best possible manner. For example, in connection with famine control, Kautilya opines that in case it is not possible for the king to manage the disaster in an appropriate manner he must relinquish and entrust the country with another more competent king [see *śloka* IV/3/17 above]. The modern rulers are to learn from this prescription of Kautilya.

Thus we see that the ancient texts may not help us in solving specific ecological and environmental problems, but they are going to give us deeper insight into the matter, which will help us solve our problems in a more harmonious way.

This is the relevance of the ancient texts like the Arthaśāstra of Kautilya for modern India and, for that matter, the modern world.

Notes

1. See Rabindranath Tagore: *Rabindra Rachanavali*, 125th Anniversary Edition:

i) Vol-2: Bharatvarsha, p.695;

ii) Vol-6: Swadeshi, p.497; Samaj, p.517; Bilaser Fans, p.526; Shiksha, p.563.

iii) Vol-7: Dharma, p.447; Shantiniketan, p.521; Tapavan, p.690.

iv) Vol-14: Palli Prakriti, p.351; Aranya Devata, p.372.

[English translations of the above text from original Bengali by the author of this article are yet to be published]

References

Santra, Prof. S.C. (ed.) (2001): *Current Perspective of Environmental Science,* Department of Environmental Science, University of Kalyani, Nadia, West Bengal.

Kangle, R. P. (1986): *Kautīlyan Arthaśāstra*, Part-II (English translation), Motilal Banarasidass, Delhi. [All quotations from Arthaśāstra in our study are from this text. In quotations, I/5/1 means Book-I, Chapter-5, *Śloka*-1 etc.]

Chapter 2. Empowerment of Women in Arthaśāstra

Introduction

One of the most important issues for which ancient Indian literature has much relevance today is women's rights and empowerment. Nowadays there is much talk about this issue. Even an International Women's Year and decade were observed. In India since independence, various show-biz measures for empowerment of women have been adopted, e.g., reservation for women in various jobs, legislative bodies etc. All these would come to naught unless measures are adopted for financial security of women, and sexual security of women is ensured by stringent punishments for sexual crime by men against women. In fact all talks of equality and rights of women without any financial security, strictly enforceable property rights, sexual security and norms preserving dignity of women are simply empty talks. In this article we are going to take up the case of property rights and financial security of women in the Arthaśāstra of Kautilya.

Financial Security of Women

In the Arthaśāstra of Kautilya, as in many other ancient Indian texts, the basis of financial security to married women was 'strīdhana' (woman's property). It consisted of landed property, jewelry, and money sufficient for maintenance of the married woman and her children. The funds were to be provided by the husband, the relatives of the husband and that of the woman who is to be married. The amount of the fund depended on the financial capabilities of the donors involved and the existing custom; but it should at least be sufficient to cover the subsistence of the woman and her children in case her husband dies, remarries or abandons her for any reason in which the woman has no fault on her part. Maintenance of 'strīdhana' was a legal compulsion and violation was subject to punishment. The state was to enforce the observance of the rules pertaining to this financial arrangement.

The following excerpt from Kautilya's� Arthaśāstra would corroborate the above observation:

III/2/14: Maintenance and ornaments constitute woman's property.

III/2/15: Maintenance is an endowment of maximum of two thousand (*panas*); as to ornaments there is no limit.

The woman can use the fund (when the husband is still there) under the following situations(and the husband may also use the fund under certain situations). To quote:

III/2/16: It is not an offence for the wife to use that for the maintenance of her sons and daughters-in-law or if no provision is made when (the husband is) away on a journey, (or) for the husband (to use it) for taking steps against robbers, diseases, famine (and other) dangers and for religious acts, or for the couple (to use it) jointly when they have begotten a son and a daughter.

The husband may, however, use the fund in the above cases only the when marriage had been a pious one. To quote:

III/2/17: And if it has been used for three years, the (wife) shall not question, in the case of the pious marriages.

III/2/18: If used in the Gāndharva and Āsura marriages, the (husband) shall be made to return both with interest, if used in the Rāksasa and Paiśāca marriages, he shall pay (the penalty for) theft.[1]

Property Rights without Remarriage

If a widow does not remarry, she would enjoy 'woman's property' until her dying day.

To quote:

III/2/19: When the husband is dead, the (widow) desirous of leading a life of piety, shall forthwith receive the endowment and ornaments and the remainder of the dowry.

III/2/33: A (widow) without sons, remaining faithful to her husband's bed, shall use her woman's property in the proximity of elders, till the end of her life.

III/2/34: For, a woman's property is meant for calamities.

After remarriage the widow generally forfeits her rights to woman's property earned in the earlier marriage. However, a widow without sons may use this property for religious purposes alone. To quote:

III/2/20: If, after receiving (these), she marries again, she shall be made to return both with interest.

III/2/26: A (widow) remarrying shall forfeit what was given her by her (late) husband.

III/2/27: She shall use it if desirous of a pious life.

A widow with sons always forfeits woman's property (from earlier marriage) after remarriage. She can use this property only for the maintenance and benefit of the sons.

To quote:

III/2/28: If a (widow) who has sons marries again, she shall forfeit her woman's property.

III/2/29: The sons, however, shall receive that woman's property.

III/2/30: Or, if she remarries for the maintenance of her sons, she shall augment (the woman's property) for the sake of the sons.

III/2/31: The (woman) shall settle on sons born (to her) from many husbands her woman's property as given by the respective fathers.

III/2/32: A (widow) marrying again shall settle on her sons her woman's property even when she is entitled to do what she pleases with it.

If a widow, without children, remarries in order to have children and a family, she may be permitted to enjoy woman's property if remarriage is done according to the likes of the earlier father-in-law's family. To quote:

III/2/21: If, however, she is desirous of having a family, she shall receive, at the time of remarriage, what was given to her by her father-in-law and her (late) husband.

III/2/23: If she remarries against the wishes of her father-in-law, she shall forfeit what was given her by her father-in-law and her (late) husband.

The wife can abandon the husband and still enjoy woman's property in the following cases:

III/2/48: A husband, who has become degraded or gone to a foreign land or has committed an offence against the king or is dangerous to her life or has become an outcast or even an impotent one may be abandoned.

Remarriage in Case of Short Absence of Husband

Kautilya clearly specifies the period for which a woman is to wait (to be permitted to remarry if she likes to do so) in case of short absence of husband for various castes and under various circumstances. To quote:

III/4/24: The wives of a *Śūdra*, a *Vaiśya*, a *Kshatriya* and a *Brāhmana*, who are away on a short journey, shall wait for a period (of one year) increased successively by one year, if they have not borne children, for one year more, if they have borne children.

III/4/25: Those who are provided for (shall wait) for double the period.

III/4/26: The trustees shall maintain those unprovided for, kinsmen for four or eight years after that.

III/4/27: Thereafter, they shall release (them) after taking back according as they had given.

III/4/28: The (wife) shall wait for a *Brāhmana* who is away studying, for ten years if she has no child, for twelve if she has a child, for a royal servant (she shall wait) till the end of her life.

III/4/29: And if she bears a child from a man of the same *varna*, she shall not incur blame.

III/4/30: Or, when the affluence of the family has disappeared, she, being released by the trustees, may marry again as she desires, or when she is in distress, for the sake of livelihood.

III/4/31: After a pious marriage, the maiden shall wait for her husband who has gone away without informing her, for seven periods if no news is heard about him, for one year if news is heard.

III/4/32: If he has gone away after informing her, she shall wait for five periods when no news is heard, for ten if news is heard.

III/4/33: If he had paid only a part of the dowry, she shall wait for three periods if there is no news, seven periods if there is news about him.

III/4/34: If he had paid the dowry (in full), (she shall wait) for five periods if there is no news, ten if there is news.

III/4/35: After that, she may remarry as she desires, with the permission of the judges.

III/4/36: 'For, frustration of the period is destruction of sacred duty', says Kautilya.

Remarriage Case of Long Absence of Husband

Kautilya also specifies the period for which a woman is to wait (to be permitted to remarry if she likes to do so) in case of long absence of husband. To quote:

III/4/37: The wife of a (man) who has gone away on a long journey or has become a wandering monk or is dead shall wait for seven periods, for one year if she has borne children.

Conditions for Remarriage if the Husband Does not Return in Time

If the husband does not return after the stipulated period and the woman is willing to marry, she can marry only certain specified relations of the husband. Otherwise the marriage would not be recognized by law and considered as adultery. To quote:

III/4/38: After that she may approach (for marriage) a full brother of the husband.

III/4/39: If there are many (such brothers, she should approach) one who is proximate (to the husband), one who is pious, one capable of maintaining her, or the youngest if without a wife.

III/4/40: In the absence of these, even one who is not a full brother, a *sapinda* or a member of the family who is near.

III/4/42: In case she marries setting aside these heirs of her husband, (or) in case she has a lover, the lover, the woman, the bestower (of the woman) and the man who marries her receive the penalty for adultery.

Inheritance of Women's Property

After the death of a woman her woman's property would be inherited by her sons and daughters (whether the husband is still alive or dead). In the absence of children, the husband, if alive, would receive a part of it and the other parts would be shared by the respective contributors. To quote:

III/2/36: If a woman dies while her husband is living, her sons and daughters shall divide her woman's property among themselves, daughters (only) if she had no sons, in the absence of these the husband (shall receive it).

III/2/37: The dowry, the post-marriage gifts and other things given by her relations, the relations shall receive.

Financial Obligations of Men to the Dependants

According to Kautilya's Arthaśāstra, it would be obligatory for a man to provide for the upkeep of his wife and children as well as parents, minor brothers, and unmarried and widowed sisters. In case he fails to discharge duties in this regard, he will be fined. He is not obliged to do these duties if anyone mentioned above [except mother], become an outcaste. It appears that he is to maintain his mother even if she becomes an outcast.

To quote:

II/1/28: If a person with means does not maintain his children and wife, his father and mother, his brothers who have not come of age, and his unmarried and widowed sisters, a fine of twelve *panas* (shall be imposed), except when these have become outcasts, with the exception of the mother.

A person desires to renounce family life to become an ascetic can do so only after he makes adequate provisions for the wife and children. And nobody should be permitted to induce a woman to renounce family life. To quote:

II/1/29: If one renounces home (to become an ascetic) without providing for his sons and wife, the lowest fine for violence (shall be imposed), also if one induces a woman to renounce home.

Relevance for Modern Times

In recent years there has been much emphasis on the empowerment of women in India. Measures like reservation of seats for women in various public bodies like the Panchayat*s*, the State Assemblies, the Parliament etc., have been undertaken. There are also legal measures against oppression of married women in the husband's family. But still there are no specific measures to ensure financial security of women, without which all other measures are likely to become meaningless.

We have seen from the discussion above that financial security of women was given top priority in the Arthaśāstra of Kautilya, particularly, the concept of 'Strīdhana' (woman's property) gives us an idea how financial security of married women till her dying day could be ensured. In fact, one undesirable aspect of western culture on our society in recent years is the inducement to disintegrate the family system, which is the building block of Indian society.

So the culture ensuring permanency of marriage is to be encouraged to obviate the harmful influence of nihilistic western culture. In this respect assurance of women's financial security is an urgent necessity. The ancient concept of woman's property, if revived (in a modified form to suit the needs of modern society), is likely to play an important role in ensuring women's financial security. This is the most mention-worthy relevance of ancient texts as regards empowerment of women.

Notes

1. Marriages according to ancient Indian texts were of eight kinds – four pious marriages and four impious marriages.

Pious Marriages

III/2/2: Making a gift of the daughter, after adorning her (with ornaments) is the Brāhma form of marriage.

III/2/3: The joint performance of sacred duties is the Prājāpatya.

III/2/4: On receiving a pair of cattle (from the bride-groom) is the Ārsa.

III/2/5: By making a gift (of the daughter) to the officiating priest inside a sacrificial altar, it is Daiva.

Impious Marriages

III/2/6: By secret association (between lovers), it is the Gāndharva.

III/2/7: On receiving a dowry, it is the Āsura.

III/2/8: By forcible seizure (of a maiden), it is the Rāksasa.

III/2/9: By the seizure of a sleeping or intoxicated (maiden), it is the Paiśāca.

References

Kangle, R. P. (1986): *Kautīlya Arthaśāstra*, Part-II (English translation), Motilal Banarasidass, Delhi.

[All quotations from Arthaśāstra in this article are from this text. In quotations I/5/1 means Book-I, Chapter-5, *Śloka*-1 etc.]

Chapter 3. Price Policy in Arthaśāstra

Introduction

A close study of ancient Indian texts, especially the Arthaśāstra of Kautilya reveals, to the surprise of the modern scholars who believe that the concept of demand and supply was generated in the West during the 18th century, that due regard was paid to demand and supply in price determination in this ancient text. The state took an active role in price determination, but state intervention in this regard had never been contrary to the market forces. Prices were to be ultimately determined on the basis of cost of production on the one hand and intensity of demand on the other. But 'Just Price', determined in this manner, was to be ensured by the state. Duty of the state in this regard was not to fix prices arbitrarily, disregarding market forces, but to see to it that traders and producers could not manipulate prices to make exorbitant profit, could not cheat the buyers or could not create crisis by taking advantage of shortages. Ancient authors, particularly *Kautilya*, were well aware of the psychology of the businessmen who, out of greed, would always distort free play of the market mechanism and charge exorbitant prices, if left alone. So the state should either determine the prices itself or approve the prices announced by the traders or producers – both on the basis of the concept of "Just Price" and paying due regard to the forces of demand and supply.

In case of temporary discrepancy [excess demand or excess supply] prices were not permitted to increase or fall, but were fixed at a given level till the discrepancy passed off. In case the discrepancy persisted, the state never attempted to keep prices rigid. In this situation, prices were increased [in case of excess demand] or reduced [in case of excess supply] step by step and by 'trial-and-error' process so as to arrive at a new equilibrium restoring balance between demand and supply. But in this regard, private persons were never given a free hand. Prices were readjusted either directly by the state, or on the basis of approval by the state the revised prices announced by the sellers. Now we examine the specific measures in this regard in the Arthaśāstra of Kautilya.

Concept of Just Price

The specific methods to fix and alter prices and the measures to implement them have been delineated in detail in the Arthaśāstra of Kautilya. According to this text, the superintendent of commerce was entrusted with the task of enforcing the price policy. The prices of different commodities were to be fixed by him. He, however, did not fix prices arbitrarily. In fact, a uniform rule was followed throughout the country to determine the 'Just Price' of each commodity. [Arthaśāstra, Book-IV, Chapter-2].

Just Price was defined as:

Just Price = Average Cost of Production + Tolls and Taxes + Transport and Associated Costs + Profit Margin.

Where,

Production Cost = Cost of Raw Materials + Wages + Interest.

In the Arthaśāstra this concept of 'Just Price' sprang directly from the ancient Indian world outlook of balance embedded in the text, according to which prices are to be so determined as to strike a balance between the interests of the buyers and that of the sellers. To fulfill this objective, the following guidelines are recommended in the Arthaśāstra.

Goods are to be sold at places specified by the state and prices should be announced [for approval by the state and knowledge of the buyers] by the businessmen. To quote:

II/22/9: "And no sale of commodities (shall be allowed) in the places of their origin."

II/21/7: "Traders shall declare the quality and price of the goods that have arrived at the foot of the flag."

Goods should bear official 'seal' and properly weighed, measured and numbered. Violation of this rule was subject to punishment. To quote:

II/21/3: "For (goods) without the stamp the penalty is double the dues."

II/21/4: "For those with a forged stamp, the fine is eight times the duty."

II/21/5: "For those with broken stamps, the penalty is distraint in the warehouse."

II/21/6: "In case of change of the royal stamp or of (change in) the name, he should make (the trader) pay a fine of one *a�pan* and a quarter per load."

II/21/15: "Therefore the sale of goods should be made by weighing; measuring or counting; an appraisal [of value should be made] of goods of small value and goods enjoying concessions."

The following *ślokas* describe the punishments for false declaration by the traders.

II/21/10: "If for fear of duty a (trader) declares the quantity of the goods or the price, to be less (than it actually is), the king shall confiscate that excess."

II/21/11: "Or the (trader) shall pay eight times the duty."

II/21/12: "He should impose the (same penalty) in case of depreciation of price of a package containing goods by (showing) a sample of lower value and in case of concealment of goods of high value by goods of low value."

Enhancement of price by bidding was discouraged. To quote:

II/21/13: "Or, if through fear of a rival purchaser a (trader) increases the price beyond the (due) price of a commodity, the king shall receive the excess in price, or make the amount of duty double."

The following *śloka* prescribes how the government officials, who took underhand means to guard the guilty merchants (accepting bribe etc.), are to be punished.

II/21/14: "The same (penalty) eightfold (shall be imposed) on the Superintendent concealing (the trader's offences)."

Components of Just Price

The Arthaśāstra of Kautilya also provides detailed guidelines for determination of various components of price as discussed below.

Wages

Guidelines for wage determination are scattered in Book-III, Chapters-13, 14; Book-IV, Chapter-2 and Book-V, Chapter-3 of the Arthaśāstra. The basic principles of wage-determination, as prescribed in these chapters, are that wages should be so determined [by contract between the employer and the employee, which once settled, would be binding on both the parties] that the employer is not cheated and at the same time the employee is not exploited. Violation of contract by either party would be subjected to punishment. Wages are to be determined on the basis of existing customs where they are available. To quote:

III/13/26: "Those who are near shall note a labourer's engagement in work."

III/13/27: "He should receive wages as agreed upon, in conformity with the work and time (if the wage is agreed upon)."

For cases, where wages are not negotiated or determined by some existing local custom, Kautilya prescribes some rules for determination wages. To quote:

III/13/28: "A cultivator, a cowherd (and) a trader should receive one-tenth part of the crops, of butter (and) of the goods dealt in by them (respectively) if the wage is not agreed upon."

III/13/29: "But if the wage is agreed upon, then as agreed upon."

III/13/30: "But the group of those who work in hope (of remuneration) such as craftsmen, artists, minstrels, physicians, professional story-tellers, attendants and others should get a remuneration as others of that type do or as experts fix."

The prescriptions for settlements of disputes regarding work are to be found in the following *ślokas*.

III/13/31: "(Disputes) shall be settled only on the testimony of witnesses."

III/13/32: "In the absence of witnesses, (the judge) should inquire at the place where the work (was carried out)."

Non-payment of wages by the employers is punishable. To quote;

III/13/33: "In the case of non-payment of wage, the fine is one-tenth or six *as�pan*."

III/13/34: "In the case of denial, the fine is twelve *as�pan* or one-fifth."

Wages in the state sector were determined in various ways. One important aspect of state sector employment of labourers is the provision of incentives through gifts etc. to the efficient labourers. To quote:

II/23/3: "He should fix the wage after ascertaining the fineness, coarseness or medium quality of the yarn, and the largeness or smallness of quantity."

II/23/4: "After finding out the amount of yarn, he should favour them with oil and myrobalan unguents."

II/23/5: "And in festive days, they should be made to work by honouring (them) and making gifts."

II/23/6: "In case of diminution in yarn, (there shall be) a diminution in wage, according to the value of the stuff."

II/23/7: "And he should cause work to be carried out by artisans producing goods with an agreement as to the amount of work, time and wage, and should maintain close contact with them."

The long list of wages of various state-sector employees as described in Book-V, Chapter-3 of the Arthaśāstra is given below.

Salaries of Government Employees

48,000 *panas* [V/3/3]: i) Sacrificial Priest; ii) Preceptor; iii) Chaplain; iv) Minister;

v) Commander-in Chief; vi) Crown Prince; vii) King's Mother; viii) Crowned Queen.

V/3/4: "With this much remuneration, they become insusceptible to instigations and disinclined to revolt."

24,000 *panas* [V/3/5]: i) Chief Palace Usher; ii) Chief Palace Guards; iii) Director (of labour corps); iv) Administrator; v) Director of stores.

V/3/6: "With this much, they become efficient in their work."

12,000 *panas* [V/3/7]: i) Princes; ii) Mothers of Princes; iii) Commandant; iv) City Judge; v) Director of Factories; vi) Provincial Officer; vii) Council of Ministers;

viii) Frontier Officer.

V/3/8: "For, with this much, they help in strengthening the entourage of the master."

8,000 *panas* [V/3/9]: i) Heads of Banded Troops; ii) Commandant of Elephants, Horses and Chariot Corps; iii) Magistrates.

V/91/3/10: "For, with this much, they are able to carry their groups with them."

4,000 *panas* [V/3/11]: i) Superintendents of Infantry, Cavalry, Chariots and Elephants

ii) Guardians of materials and Elephant-forests.

2,000 *panas* [V/3/12]: i) Chariot-fighter; ii) Elephant-trainer; ii) Physician; iii) Horse-trainer; iv) Carpenter; v) Breeders of Animals.

1,000 *panas* [V/3/13]: i) Fortune-teller; ii) Soothsayer; iii) Astrologer; iv) Narrator of *Purānas*; v) King's Charioteer [V/3/21]; vi) Bard; vii) Chaplain's Men; iii) All Superintendents; ix) Sharp Pupils, Monks Fallen from Vow, and Agents Appearing as House-holders, Traders and Ascetics [V/3/22]

500-1,000 *panas* according to merit [V/3/13]: i) Teachers and Learned Men;

ii) Elephant Driver; iii) Sorcerer; iv) Miners of Mountains; v) All kinds of Attendants, Teachers & Learned Men; vi) Spies.

250 *panas* [V/3/14]: i) Foot-soldiers trained in the (fighting) arts; ii) Groups of Accountants, clerks and others; iii) Makers of Musical Instruments [V/3/15]; iv) Village Servants, Secret Agents, Assassins, Poison-givers and Female Mendicants [V/3/23].

250 *panas* [V/3/15]: i) Actors; ii) Those moving about for Spying [V/91/3/24].

120 *panas* [V/3/16]: i) Artisans; ii) Artists.

60 *panas* [V/3/17]: i) Servants, valets, attendants and guards of Quadrupeds and Bipeds

ii) Foremen of Labourers; iii) All Attendants; iv) Riders, Bandits and Mountain-diggers supervised by *Āryas*.

10 *panas/yojana* up to 10 *yojanas* and 20 *panas/yojana* beyond 10 *yojanas*

[V/3/19]: i) The Average Envoy.

Interest

Interest rates are to be rigidly fixed by the state [considering the degree of risk involved] so as to prevent usury and exploitation of the weak borrowers. To quote:

III/11/1: "One *pana* and a quarter is the lawful rate of interest per month on one hundred *panas*, five *panas* for purposes of trade, ten *panas* for those going through forests, twenty *panas* for those going by sea."

III/11/2: "For one charging or making another charge a rate beyond that, the punishment shall be the lowest fine for violence, for witnesses, each one of them, half the fine."

III/11/3: "If, however, the king is unable to ensure protection, the (judge) should take into consideration the usual practice among creditors and the debtors."

III/11/4: "Interest on grains (shall be) up to a half, on the harvesting crops; thereafter it may increase being turned into capital."

III/11/5: "Interest on capital (shall amount to) half the profit, to be paid for one year, being set apart in a store."

From the above excerpts it turns out that annual interest rates for various categories of borrowers were:

For Non-Commercial Loans = 15%

For Less Risky Commercial Loans = 60%

For Risky Commercial Loans = 120% and

For Foreign Trade = 240%.

If we closely look at the above chart, it is found that the rate of interest on loans for foreign trade (24% per annum) was much higher than that on loans for internal trade. This is quite contrary to the present day state policy pursued in India where, considering the chronic balance of payments crisis, it is desirable that interest on loans for foreign trade, esp. for exports, should be lower than that on loans for internal trade. The most feasible explanation for highest rate of interest for foreign trade lies in the risk factor in different kind of loans. In those days transport and communication systems were undeveloped. So, foreign trade was much more hazardous than internal trade. In those days, modern commercial banks and lending institutions were non-existent and most of the private money-lenders were not much resourceful. So, risk factor used to play a dominant role in determining the rate of interest. If we look closely t the chart for interest rates above, it is found that even in case of internal trade, interest rate increases according to the degree of hazards involved in trading. Interest rate on loans for hazardous internal trade (120% per annum) is double of that on loans for hazard-free internal trade (60% per annum). By the same logic one may conclude that interest rate on loans for foreign trade, which involved much more hazards (than internal trade), would be higher in general as compared to interest rates on loans for internal trade.

Profit

Profit rate is also to be rigidly fixed by the state so as to avoid uncertainty and to prevent traders from profiteering. There are also specific guidelines for ascertaining transport, storage and other associated expenses. Rigid and simplified rules are to be observed for determining tolls and taxes on all the commodities produced and traded. Higher profit rate is permissible for foreign trade. The following extract is relevant in this regard.

IV/2/28: "And he should fix a profit for them of five per hundred over and above the permitted purchase price in case of indigenous commodities; ten (per hundred) in case of foreign goods."

Any trader, trying to earn a higher profit than prescribed by the state, will be punished.

To quote:

IV/2/29: "For those who increase the price beyond that or secure (a profit beyond that) during purchase or sale, the fine shall be two hundred *panas* for (an additional profit of) five *as�pan* in one hundred *paṇas*."

Implementation

Price policy in the Arthaśāstra was inexorably associated with the methods of implementation, which consisted of: (a) Administrative measures; (b) Accounting; and (c) Buffer stock.

Administrative Measures

As regards implementation of price policy, a crucial role was played by the superintendent of the toll house. Simultaneously with collection of tolls, he was entrusted with the task of implementing prices fixed by the superintendent of commerce. If the concerned officials shirked their duties or adopted corrupt practices in connivance with the traders, they were punished [see II/21/14 at the end of section-II].

The espionage network used to play an important role in the implementation of price policy. False statements regarding costs and prices, adulteration, smuggling, overvaluation, under-valuation, etc. by the merchants, could not have been prevented without the help of the spies.

Government officials, entrusted with the task of implementing price policy, could not resort to corrupt practices as spies in different guises were looming at every corner. Anybody, whatever is his apparent identity, may be a disguised spy and so, the fear of being detected and punished discouraged merchants and government officials to resort to underhand practices by violating rules and procedures of price control laid down by the state. To quote:

II/21/17: "Secret agents operating on roads and in places without roads should find out such (evasion)."

II/21/27: "Or a secret agent appearing as a trader should communicate to the king the size of the caravan."

As regards the ubiquitous nature of the espionage network of Kautilya, a modern author opines:

"There were spies in every traders' caravan." [Kosambi 1981, P.147]

The espionage network facilitated perfect implementation of price policy by ensuring: (i) Dissemination of correct information relevant to costs and prices, and (ii) Prevention of corruption.

Accounting

Detailed and accurate methods of accounting and auditing, as delineated in Arthaśāstra of Kautilya, reminds one of the accounting methods of a highly developed capitalist economy. Salaries of all the state employees should be paid promptly, all state orders should be in writing, power and duties of all the state departments should be clearly defined, separate registers should be maintained for every item and accounts should be regularly entered in prescribed registers. In Chapter 7 of Book II of the *Arthaśāstra*, the functions of the Superintendent of Audit and Accounts are prescribed in the following manner.

II/7/1: "The Superintendent should cause the Record Office to be built facing the east or the north, with separate halls, (as) a place for record books."

II/7/2: "There he should cause to be entered in the record-books: the extent of the number, activity and total (income) of the departments; the amount of increase or decrease in the use of the (various) materials, expenses, excess, surcharge, mixing, place, wages and labourers in connection with factories; the price, the quality, the weight, the measure, the height, the depth and the container in connection with jewels, articles of high value, of low value and forest produce; laws, transactions, customs and fixed rules of regions, villages, castes, families and corporations; the receipt of favours, lands, use, exemptions, and food and wages by those who serve the king; the receipt of jewels and land (and), the receipt of special allowances and (payments for) remedial measures against sudden calamities, by the king and his queens and sons; and payments and receipts in connection with peace and war with allies and enemies."

II/7/3: "From that he should hand over in writing the (revenue) estimate, accrued revenue, outstanding revenue, income and expenditure, balance, (the time for) attendance (for audit), (sphere of) activity, customs and fixed rules, to all the departments."

As regards the functions of the officers of different departments pertaining to auditing of the records of the respective departments, Kautilya prescribes the following guidelines.

II/7/16: "The accounts should come in on *Āsādha* full moon day."

II/7/17: "When the (officers) have come with sealed account books and balances in sealed containers, he should impose restriction in one place, not allowing conversation (among them)."

II/7/18: "After hearing the totals of income, expenditure and balance, he should cause the balance to be taken away (to the treasury)."

II/7/21: "For (officers) not coming at the proper time or coming without the account-books and balances, the fine shall be one-tenth of the amount due."

II/7/22: "And if, when the works officer presents himself, the accounts officer is not ready to audit, the lowest fine for violence (shall be imposed)."

II/7/23: "In the reverse case, the fine for the works officer (shall be) double."

II/7/24: "The high officers should render accounts in full in accordance with their activity, without contradicting themselves."

II/7/25: "And among these he who makes a divergent statement or speaks falsely shall pay the highest fine (for violence)."

The account books of different departments are to be presented in full before the audit officer in time. In case of delay due to unavoidable circumstances, some concessions in this regard may be made, but up to a certain limit. To quote:

II/7/26: "He should wait for one month, if the (officer) has not brought in the day-to-day accounts."

II/7/27: "After the month, the (officer) shall pay a fine of two hundred *as�pan* increased (by that amount) for each succeeding month."

II/7/28: "If an (officer) has a little of written balance due (from him), he should wait for five days."

II/7/29: "If he brings in the day-to-day accounts after that period, preceded by (delivery of the balance into) the treasury, he should look into (the case) with reference to laws, transactions, customs and fixed rules and by totaling up, (and by looking at) the work actually carried out, by inference and the use of spies."

The guidelines of checking up the accounts by the audit and accounts officer are prescribed in the following *ślokas*.

II/7/30: "And he should check (the accounts) for each day, group of five days, fortnight, month, four months and year."

II/7/31: "He should check the income with reference to the period, place, time, head of income, source, bringing forward, quantity, the payer, the person causing payment to be made, the recorder and the receiver."

II/7/32: "He should check the expenditure with reference to the period, place, time, head (of expenditure), gain, occasion, the thing given, its use and amount, the person who orders, the person who takes out, the person who delivers and the receiver."

II/7/33: "He should check the balance with reference to the period, place, time, head, bringing forward, the article, its characteristics, amount, the vessel in which it is deposited and the person guarding it."

The restrictions on the accounts officer and various punitive measures against him, in case he fails to discharge his assigned duties in a proper way, are prescribed in the following *ślokas*.

II/7/34: "If, in an affair of the king, the accounts officer is not ready for audit or disregards an order or changes the income and expenditure in a way different from the written order, the lowest fine for violence (shall be imposed)."

II/7/35: "For one writing down an item (in the accounts) without any order or in a wrong order or in an illegible manner, or twice over, the fine is twelve *panas*."

II/7/36: "For one writing down the balance (in any of these ways) the fine is double (that)."

II/7/39: "In case of a false statement, the punishment is that for theft."

II/7/40: "For admitted afterwards, (the fine is) double, so also if an item is forgotten and then brought in."

The process of maintaining accounts by the Director of Stores is prescribed in the following *śloka*.

II/5/22: "He should be conversant with receipts from outside and inside even after a hundred years, so that when asked he would not falter in respect of expenditure, balance and collections."

The following *ślokas* contain prescriptions for inspection of the works of the officers of different government departments.

II/9/19: "Therefore, he who is appointed by an order to a particular department shall communicate to him [i.e., the king] the real nature of that work and the income and expenditure (both) in detail and in the aggregate."

II/9/28: "Therefore, his superintendents should carry out the works accompanied by accountants, writers, examiners of coins, receivers of balance and supervisors."

Buffer Stock

In the Arthaśāstra much emphasis is laid on the maintenance of a buffer stock of all commodities so as to meet accidental shortages and thus, to ensure smooth implementation of the price policy. To quote:

II/15/22: "From these he should set apart one half for times of distress for the country people, (and) use the (other) half for times of distress for the country people, (and) use the (other) half."

II/15/23: "And he should replace old (stock) with new."

Relevance for Modern Times

The price policy in the Arthaśāstra was basically designed for monarchy. So, the question arises if it has any relevance for the democratic India today. If we closely study the price policy in the Arthaśāstra and the suggested measures to implement them, it would be clear that none of them is contradictory to the provisions of the Constitution of democratic India today. In fact it sprang from the basic Indian world outlook of balance and harmony. Price control is necessary to ensure this harmony because activities associated with profit and accumulation of wealth inherently contains the unbalancing factor of 'greed'. So unless restrained by the state, pricing by traders and producers would automatically generate disharmony. So, whatever be the form of the government, it must run, according to the ancient Indian world outlook, in conformity with *dharma* and should impose *dharma* on all material activities [pursuits of *artha* and *kāma*] to assure harmony and balance. This is a basic outlook and not conditioned by the form of the government.

As regards the necessity of price-control in India today, L.K.Jha, the ex-Governor of the Reserve Bank of India, pointed out that prices in an LDC like India cannot be left to be determined by market forces where, instead of free competition, monopolistic control prevails.

Direct price-control becomes necessary in India, according to Jha, for the following reasons:

(i) To protect the interests of the vulnerable sections of the population;

(ii) To guide investment to the desired channels; and

(iii) To prevent hoarders from increasing prices by taking advantage of shortages.

[Jha, 1968, PP. 478-80]

Thus we se that in spite of the differences in the political systems, the basic objective of ancient Indian price policy resemble the 'administered price-policy' under the Five-Year Plans in India. But the ancient Indian price policy distinguishes itself for the following reasons:

(i) Unlike in India today, monetary and fiscal policies were not used for price control in ancient India. Only direct price-control measures were applied.

(ii) Unnecessary controls were always avoided in ancient India.

(iii) Prices were rigidly fixed by the state only when discrepancies between demand and supply were temporary. In case of persistent discrepancies, prices were permitted to vary according to market forces of demand and supply. But even in such a case, suitable adjustments were made by the state or, revised prices proposed by the sellers were to be approved by the state. Private sellers were never permitted to do such revisions on their own.

(iv) Price policy was accompanied by suitable administrative and legal measures for its proper implementation.

The basic outcomes of price-policy pursued in India during the plan period were:

(i) Administered prices for various agricultural and industrial commodities;

(ii) Vast subsidies arising out of the endeavour to fulfill simultaneously the contradictory objectives of providing price incentives to the producers and provision of low-priced essential goods to the consumers.

The above features, however, have led to many undesirable effects on the Indian Economy. The Seventh and Eighth Plan Documents [Planning Commission], various issues of the Report on Currency and Finance [RBI], and Economic Survey [Government of India] have revealed many disquieting features of the administered price policy in India. In fact, instead of having control over the prices, the price-controlling authorities are themselves being controlled by extraneous forces, which compel them to raise prices in inappropriate moments leading to many adverse repercussions on the economy. So to avoid the adverse impacts of a badly conceived and badly managed price policy and to devise a proper price policy, the government of India at present can take the following lessons from the ancient texts, particularly, the Arthaśāstra of Kautilya.

(i) The market mechanism should not be interfered with unnecessarily. The government should interfere only when it is necessary, e.g., when monopolies or vested-interest groups try to obstruct the smooth functioning of the market mechanism, when traders and hoarders try to complicate the situation of shortage and fish out of troubled water, etc.

(ii) There should be appropriate administrative and legal set up for proper implementation of the price policy, as in the Arthaśāstra. We may tone up our administrative and legal systems and emulate many features of the Arthaśāstra- Economy in this regard, without violating any provisions of our democratic political set up.

One strong objection against Kautilya's measures is related to the exhaustive espionage network of Kautilya. This may be contrary to ideal democratic norms. But, an efficient intelligence network is necessary under all systems to maintain administrative efficiency and to suppress corruption. Secret agencies like the CBI [Central Bureau of Investigations], Intelligence Branch, Special Branch, Enforcement

Branch, Vigilance Departments etc., are essential for proper functioning of the government, and to fight crime and corruption. No patriotic person is likely to consider the CBI's actions against the unscrupulous politicians undemocratic. Moreover, the vast Espionage Network of Kautilya was an alternative to the quick transport and communication facilities, which Kautilya's spies could be easily handled by computers and the Internet.

So it is likely that emulation of these basic features of ancient Indian price policy would convert our ill-administered price policy under planning into a well-administered one, which would be capable of restoring balance in the market mechanism, facilitating unhindered functioning of the market mechanism, and bringing about welfare of the majority of the population of the country.

It is desirable that prices of most of the commodities are to be determined by the forces of the market. But prices of some sensitive commodities are to be fixed and directly regulated by the state. At present the list of commodities for administered pricing are haphazardly selected, and at times, to at the behest of the vested interest groups. This is not at all desirable. The question is one of selecting the appropriate commodities for which prices are to be administered by the state.

References

Government of India: *Economic Survey*, Various issues

Government of India, Planning Commission: *7th, 8th and 9th Plans.*

Jha, L.K. (1968): "Price Policy in a Developing Economy", *Reserve Bank of India Bulletin*, April.

Kangle, R. P. (1986): *Kautiliya Arthaśāstra*, Part-II [English translation], Motilal Banarasidass, Delhi. [All quotes are from this translation; in quotes II/1/3 means Book-2, Chapter-1, *Śloka*-3].

Kosambi, D.D. (1981): *The Culture and Civilization of Ancient India*, Vikas Publishing House, New Delhi.

Mukherjee, Bharati (1976): *Kautilya's Concept of Diplomacy*, Minerva Associates Pvt. Ltd., Calcutta.

Reserve Bank of India: *Report on Currency and Finance*, Various issues.

Chapter 4. Gandhian Concept of Swadeshi

Introduction

One of the central points of Gandhian economic thought was the concept of Swadeshi.

After independence, the Nehru group eschewed the Gandhian Path and accepted the

Stalinist Path of Industrialization in modified form and thus the concept of Swadeshi

went completely into oblivion. In course of the worldwide awareness as regards the

necessity of attaching 'Human Face' to the process of globalization, the concept of

Swadeshi has once again come to the fore. In course of planning in India, stress was laid,

especially since the Second Five Year Plan, on development of large scale basic and capital goods industries on the basis of Mahalanobis Strategy of industrialization. This was akin to the Socialistic (Stalinist?) pattern of industrialization. As a result, in course of only a few decades, India could achieve a mention worthy large scale industrial sector. But this sector did not play any trickle down effect to remove the problems of unemployment and poverty.

However, the existence of the state sector could provide some safety net. Then in the arly nineties, India adopted the policy of liberalization, globalization and privatization. Doors of import of foreign capital and technology were opened. But the adverse impact of this new economic policy on economic conditions of the majority of the population and on ecology and environment could be felt only a decade after the adoption of the new policy. Worse was the case of the employment situation. Supply of labour force went on increasing because of high rate of growth of population, but the rate of job creation in the organized sector started falling. Agricultural sector has already been over-burdened with the pressure of population, and because of the large-industry- biased policies, there has been continuous degeneration of the small and tiny sectors and thus rate of employment generation in the unorganized sector as a whole is also declining. All these have made the unemployment problem grave.

Now there has arisen the problem of large scale exodus of the peasants as a consequence of acquisition of agricultural lands for establishment of large scale industries. This is a very serious problem and has resulted in social tensions and peasant revolts, especially in West Bengal, where "industrialization" as such, without considering its adverse impact on employment, poverty and ecology, has become the basic political slogan of the ruling party.

In brief, industrialization process in India at present has revealed all its demonic features.

Now the matter has drawn attention of the thoughtful persons and the question has arisen if it is possible to endow a human face to the process of industrialization under the new scenario of globalization. In this context the Gandhian concept of Swadeshi has once again come to the fore. It is true that objective conditions, since Gandhiji devised the concept, have changed significantly. Still the concept in its essence may play an important role in resolving the trade off between industrialization and welfare of the majority. Underlying the concept of Swadeshi is the spirit of industrial development based on the efforts of the masses and locally available technology and catering to the needs of the majority without at the same time obstructing the establishment of modern industries and import of sophisticated foreign technology wherever they are really essential. The concept of Swadeshi also indirectly takes into account the question of preserving environment and ecology. To go into these matters in detail and to consider their relevance for the present day problems, we are to define first the concept of Swadeshi as conceived by Mahatma Gandhi.

Definition of Swadeshi

The common definition of Swadeshi as came out of the works of Gandhiji is use of all home-made products to the exclusion of foreign products which are not beneficial to the people of the country and harmful on the contrary. To quote:

"The broad definition of Swadeshi is the use of all home-made things to the exclusion of foreign things, in so far as such use is necessary for protection of home-industry, more especially those industries without which India will become pauperized. In my opinion, therefore, Swadeshi which excludes the use of everything foreign, because it is foreign, no matter how beneficial it may be, and irrespective of the fact that it impoverishes nobody, is a narrow interpretation of Swadeshi."[1]

Swadeshi, defined in this manner, has far reaching significance as regards removal of poverty and unemployment, upgrading the skills of the masses, encouraging their creative powers, inculcating the spirit of self help and self confidence in them regarding their own powers (without approaching the authorities, begging bowls in hand) to change their own fate and also supply of mass consumption goods. Swadeshi, if practiced properly, would prevent wastage of resources available within the country and frittering away of these resources to the production of goods catering to the needs of the foreigners or luxury needs of the well to do minority within the country at the cost of production of mass consumption goods. Gandhiji rightly emphasized that departure from Swadeshi and blind rush for foreign goods and technology was the basic cause of mass poverty in India. To quote:

"Much of the deep poverty of the masses is due to the ruinous departure from Swadeshi in the economic and industrial life."[2]

Gandhiji suggests that there are still innumerable rural industries, which are capable of

catering to the needs of the masses and at the same time creating significant employment

opportunities. These industries are at present unable to play their roles properly because of the lack of assistance in terms of organization, training, supply of quality raw materials, technology up gradation etc. and above all, competition from the large industries and imported foreign goods boosted up by the pro-rich policy of the government. To quote:

"In that of economics, I should use only things that are produced by my immediate

neighbours and serve those industries by making them efficient and complete where they

might be found wanting. It is suggested that such Swadeshi, if reduced to practice, will lead to the millennium, because we do not expect quite to reach it within our times, so may we not abandon Swadeshi even though it may not be fully attained for generations to come."[3]

"If we follow the Swadeshi doctrine, it would be your duty and mine to find out neighbours who can supply our wants and to teach them to supply them where they do not know how to proceed, assuming that there are neighbours who are in want of healthy occupation."[4]

Gandhiji had already realized that agriculture was under much pressure and considering the number of peasants vis-à-vis total available cultivable land, agriculture alone could hardly provide sustenance to the innumerable poor peasants. Here cottage industries are likely to play the role of subsidiary occupation to the small cultivators. To quote:

"So, when we find that there are many things that we cannot get in India, we must try to do without them."[5]

"Swadeshi, therefore, is the problem of inducing and enabling the farmers to take up the

supplementary industry of spinning and weaving."[6]

"Without a cottage industry, the Indian peasant is doomed. He cannot maintain himself

from the produce of the land. He needs a supplementary industry. Spinning is the easiest,

the cheapest and the best."[7]

"Swadeshi, therefore is a question of finding a subsidiary industry for our farmers."[8]

Swadeshi in the form of revival of the cottage and rural industries also has an indirect

beneficial effect, besides employment and income generation and supply of mass

consumption goods. Works in cottage industries require inculcation of individual skill and therefore small and cottage industries improve mental faculty of the artisans. On the other hand, mechanistic jobs with machines in large scale industries stultify mental and creative faculties of the wage labourers. Development of mental faculties of the masses through the rural industries would enable them to be organized on the basis of self help, fellow feeling, self confidence and self respect. To quote:

"I swear by Swadeshi as it affords occasion for an ample exercise of all our faculties, and as it tests every one of the millions of men and women, young and old. It can succeed only if India acts as one mind. And if India can do so in Swadeshi, she will have learnt the secret of Swaraj. She will then have mastered the art of destruction and construction in a scientific manner."[9]

Because of age-old suffering and deprivation, rural masses are languishing in the darkness of resignation and fatalism. So it is the duty of the educated and cultured people to instill the spirit of confidence among the masses by themselves directly participating in the practice of Swadeshi. To quote:

"We will have experts and chemists who will be prepared to place their knowledge at the

disposal of the villagers. We will, through our experts, offer to test the articles

manufactured by village handicraftsmen and make them suggestions to improve their

wares."[10]

"In other words, we should evoke the artistic talent of the villager."[11]

"It provides limitless work for the creative genius in the country." [12]

"The condition of success is that cultured men and women take up spinning and weaving.

The people will follow their example."[13]

Gandhiji opines that the spirit of neither nationalism nor internationalism could be

inculcated unless 'charity begins at home', i.e., unless one begins from concern and fellow feeling for the immediate neighbors. This spirit of fellow feeling and service mentality for the neighbors would gradually rise upwards to generate a true feeling of nationalism and internationalism. Talks of internationalism without any concern for the neighbors are sheer falsehood and hypocrisy. To quote:

"If this interpretation of Swadeshi be correct, then it follows that its votary will, as a first

duty, dedicate himself to the service of his immediate neighbours. This involves exclusion or even sacrifice of the interests of the rest, but the exclusion or the sacrifice would be only in appearance. Pure service of our neighbours can never, from its very nature, result in disservice to those who are far away, but rather the contrary." [14]

"Therefore, one who serves his neighbour serves all the world."[15]

To start with Gandhiji's Swadeshi had its central point Khadi, i.e., cotton textiles of the

craft industries. The reason is very simple. The industry which had the widest coverage, in terms of both demand and supply, was Khadi. So Gandhiji attached highest priority to this age-old industry. At the same time he did not fail to emphasize that besides Khadi, other traditional rural industries should also be revived. To quote:

"But Khadi is not the only such struggling industry. I, therefore, suggest to you to direct

your attention and effort to all the small-scale, minor, unorganized industries that are today

in need of public support. They may be wiped out if no effort is made in their behalf. Some of these are being pushed back by large-scale industries which flood the markets with their manufactures. It is these that cry for help." [16]

"We must promote every useful industry that was existent a short while ago, and the

extinction of which has now resulted in unemployment." [17]

"Our clear duty is, therefore, to investigate the possibility of keeping in existence the village wheel, the village crusher and the village pounder, and, by advertising their products, discovering their qualities, ascertaining the condition of the workers and the number displaced by the power-driven machinery and discovering the methods of improving them, whilst retaining their village character, to enable them to stand the competition of the mills." [18]

"There are numberless other village, and even town, crafts that need public support, if they are to live and thus maintain the thousands of poor artisans depending upon them for their daily bread." [19]

Gandhiji had observed with concern that the plans and economic policies of the government were directed at extracting resources from the rural sector to cater to the needs of the foreign industries and well-to-do minority in the cities. He strongly suggested that this process should be discontinued forthwith and Swadeshi is the best means to do so.

To quote:

"whereas, at the present moment, we are exploiting the villagers without making any return worth the name."[20]

"This is much more impossible than the one of reviving the village industries and stopping the progressive poverty, which is due as much to enforced unemployment as to any other cause."[21]

"But I heartily endorse the proposition that any plan, which exploits the raw materials of country and neglects the potentially more powerful man-power, is lopsided and can never tend to establish human equality." [22]

"Therefore, real planning consists in the best utilization of the whole man-power of India,

and the distribution of the raw products of India in her numerous villages instead of sending them outside and reburying finished articles at fabulous prices."[23]

Economic and Ethical Aspects

Gandhiji's economic thought has the unique characteristics that it is inexorably associated

with his ethical and religious norms and is a part of his living. Gandhiji strongly points out that conventional economics based on gratification of selfish ends is highly unethical and immoral and contrary to his own economic thinking based on philanthropy and ethics. Thus while defining Swadeshi Gandhiji does not fail to point out its religious and moral aspects.To quote:

"Swadeshi, as defined here, is a religious discipline to be undergone in utter disregard of

the physical discomfort it may cause to individuals."[24]

Claiming to serve foreigners in the name of internationalism is highly immoral according to Gandhiji. To quote:

"I cannot starve my neighbour and claim to serve my distant cousin in the North Pole. This is the basic principle of all religions, and we will find it is also of true and humane

economics."[25]

Economics that encourages one country to exploit another is also unethical. To quote:

"Economics that hurt the moral well-being of an individual or a nation are immoral and,

herefore, sinful. Thus, the economics that permit one country to prey upon another are

immoral. It is sinful to buy and use articles made by sweated labour. It is sinful to eat

American wheat and let my neighbour, the grain dealer, starve for want of custom." [26]

"That economics is untrue which ignores or disregards moral values."[27]

"The economics that disregard moral and sentimental considerations are like wax works,

that, being life–like, still lack the life of the living flesh. At every crucial moment, these

new-fangled economic laws have broken down in practice. And nations or individuals who accept them as guiding maxims must perish." [28]

Gandhiji also points out clearly that economic ideas developed under the objective

conditions of one country may not be suitable for other countries with different set of

objective conditions. Unfortunately economists and policy makers of our country have

failed to realize the essence of this view of Gandhiji even today. Gandhiji specifically

mentions the case of free trade in this respect. Unrestricted free trade is beneficial for the

developed countries but they are likely to have serious adverse consequences for the

developing countries like India. Here lies the seed of economic thinking that flourished

later in writings of Neo-Marxists like Raul Prebisch, Singer etc. To quote:

"The economics of a nation are determined by its climate, geological and temperamental

conditions. The Indian conditions are different from the English in all these essentials"[29]

Swadeshi and Large Scale Industries

Gandhiji goes into the pros and cons of the operation of the large scale industries and

dispels the false belief that use of cloth produced by mills owned by Indians is also

Swadeshi. Mills, whatever is the ownership, use mainly imported raw materials and thereby assist employment and income generation in exporter countries, not in India. To quote:

"Thousands of men believe that by using cloth woven in Indian mills, they comply with the requirements of the Swadeshi vow. The fact is that most fine cloth is made out of foreign cotton, spun outside India. Therefore, the only satisfaction to be derived from the use of such cloth is that it is woven in India."[30]

"Even on handlooms for very fine cloth only foreign yarn is used. The use of such cloth

does not amount to an observance of Swadeshi. To say so, is simple self-deception."[31]

According to Gandhiji, mills are solely guided by profit motive and not the interest of the

wellbeing of the masses. On the contrary they won't hesitate to exploit the masses if

earning of profit warrants so. To quote:

"It is my firm belief that mills, by reason of the limitations under which they must work,

will fail us in the end if we rely upon them. Then, they being concerns predominantly for

making profits irrespective of national considerations, will not scruple to exploit the public and even to sell foreign cloth as Swadeshi."[32]

"The only thing they reluctantly contribute is to employ cheap labour of the country and make a gullible public believe that these are Swadeshi concerns."[33]

Large scale industries are based on mechanization and indiscriminate development of such industries would have harmful effect on the Indian economy with a vast body of

unemployed. Gandhiji explains how mills generate fewer jobs than they are likely to

displace and thereby aggravate the unemployment situation. To quote:

"Mechanization is good when the hands are too few for the work intended to be

accomplished. It is an evil when then are more hands than required for the work, as is the

case in India."[34]

Mill-made cloth may be cheaper and the difference of price between mill-made cloth and

handloom-cloth may be a considered as a social gain. But if looked more closely, it would be found that the social cost of additional unemployment created by the mills would far outweigh this paltry gain derived from lower price. Here Gandhiji dwells upon the concept of Negative Externalities of large scale production. To quote:

"For, if they have displaced thousands of workers, the cheapest mill cloth is dearer than the dearest Khadi woven in the villages." [35]

"Strange as it may appear, every mill generally is a menace to the villagers. I have

notworked out the figures, but I am quite safe in saying that every mill-hand does the work of at least ten laborers doing the same work in their villages. In other a words he earns more than he did in his village at the expense of ten fellow-villagers."[36]

Gandhiji did not deny the importance of large scale industries in essential spheres like basic and capital goods. But they are to be developed only as complementary to small scale and cottage industries, not as rivals. Moreover he opines tat these large industries should be centralized in industrial centers alone and should not be permitted to penetrate the rural sector indiscriminately. Probably, he had in mind the ecological question besides the adverse effect on rural economy and culture. To quote:

"Heavy industries will necessarily be centralized and nationalized. But they will occupy the least part of the vast national activity in the villages."[37]

Swadeshi and Foreign Trade

It is a commonly held wrong impression that the concept of Swadeshi is against all foreign goods, capital and technology. This is highly erroneous. Gandhiji was well aware that for an industrially backward country like India, foreign trade, foreign capital and foreign technology may be essential in certain fields. But it is to be seen that they are not resorted to indiscriminately to cater to the needs of foreign business and luxury consumption of the rich minority at the cost of the majority and environment. For a poor country like India, unrestricted free trade would only serve the interests of England and other developed nations, and the luxury requirements of the native rich. The same is the case for foreign capital and technology if permitted without any restriction and consideration of the wellbeing of the masses. Gandhiji here makes clear that imports of foreign goods, capital and technology should be strictly restricted to areas where they are essential and where they are likely to serve the interests of the majority and future economic prospect of the country. They should never be permitted to destroy local industries and employment opportunities. Gandhiji points out that free trade was the root cause of economic bondage of India.

To quote:

"Free trade for India has proved her curse and held her in bondage."[38]

"India was enslaved for satisfying the greed of the foreign cloth manufacturer. When the

East India Company came in, we were able of manufacture all the cloth we needed and

more for export. By processes that need not be described here, India has become practically wholly dependent upon foreign manufacture for her clothing."[39]

"We forget that what may be perfectly good for certain conditions in the West is not

necessarily good for certain other, and often diametrically opposite, conditions in the East. Free trade, which may have been good enough for England, would certainly have ruined Germany. Germany prospered only because her thinkers, instead of slavishly following, England took note of the special conditions of their own land, and devised economics suited to them."[40]

He clarifies why free trade which is beneficial for developed countries like England is not

so for a poor country like India. To quote:

"The economics of a nation are determined by its climate, geological and temperamental

conditions. The Indian conditions are different from the English in all

these essentials"[41]

"A country remains poor in wealth, both material and intellectual, if it does not develop its handicrafts and its industries and lives a lazy parasitic life by importing all the

manufactured articles from outside."[42]

"The process is now reversed and we are dependent upon the outside world for most

manufactured goods."[43]

Gandhiji cites examples how free trade was responsible for destruction of indigenous industries and aggravation of the employment situation in India. To quote:

"The Lancashire cloth, as English historians have shown, was forced upon India, and her own world-famed manufactures were deliberately and systematically ruined." [44]

"Many weavers have become sweepers. Some have taken to the profession of hired soldiers. Half the race of artistic weavers has died out, and the other half is weaving imported foreign yarn for want of finer hand-spun yarn." [45]

"But free trade has ruined India's peasantry in that it has all but destroyed her cottage industry. Moreover, no new trade can compete with foreign trade without protection."[46]

He strongly dispels the misgiving that he is blindly against all foreign goods. He welcomes import of foreign goods where they are essential for the benefit of the nation and its people.

To quote:

"All British goods do not harm us. Some goods, such as English books, we need for our intellectual of spiritual benefit."[47]

"In my opinion, therefore, Swadeshi which excludes the use of everything foreign, because it is foreign, no matter how beneficial it may be, and irrespective of the fact that it impoverishes nobody, is a narrow interpretation of Swadeshi."[48]

"Swadeshi admits of and welcomes the introduction of all foreign goods that cannot or need not be manufactured in India and that would benefit her people. Thus Swadeshi

admits all foreign books containing pure literature, all foreign watches, foreign needles,

foreign sewing machines, foreign pins." [49]

He also opines that guarantee of security of all beneficial foreign companies and honest

foreign citizen is a part of Swadeshi.

"I would guarantee the fullest protection for every European living in India and all hones

European Enterprises."[50]

"To reject foreign manufactures merely because they are foreign, and to go on wasting

national time and money to promote manufactures in one's country for which it is not

suited, would be criminal folly and a negation of the Swadeshi spirit. A true votary of

Swadeshi will never harbour ill-will towards the foreigner, he will not be actuated by

antagonism towards anybody on earth. Swadeshism is not a cult of hatred. It is a doctrine

of selfless service, that has its roots in the purest Ahimsa, i.e., love."[51]

"There is no harm in importing raw material when it cannot be found in India."[52]

Relevance for Modern Times

Globalization in India has at present manifested in the form of blind craze for establishment of large scale industries based on imported and unaltered foreign technology and capital at any cost. The matter has taken a horrible turn in West Bengal revealing all the demonic features of globalization. There are lengthy processions and street meetings organized by the ruling party and with party toughs clamoring nerve rending slogans: "Industrialization is a must and anyone opposing it would be crushed ruthlessly." The Nandigram and Singur episodes of successful mass resistance against displacement of poor cultivators by party goons under police coverage has once again brought to the fore the question of assigning human face to the process of globalization and need to devise methods of industrialization not to serve the interests of foreign MNCs and luxury needs of native well to do minority, but the interest of the nation and wellbeing of the majority of its population, and preservation of environment and ecology. In this regard the Gandhian concept of Swadeshi as defined above comes to the fore.

Establishment of large scale industries with unaltered foreign technology would serve the interests of the foreign MNCs and their domestic counterparts, and the native well to do minority at the cost of the majority by aggravating unemployment situation through takeover of agricultural land displacing poor cultivators and destruction of rural craft industries. They will also have irreparable adverse impact on environment and ecology and the culture in the country side.

In general, overall employment elasticity of the highly capital-intensive modern sector is low compared to that of the craft industries and small industries. [Sen, Abhijit 1996]. All the studies reveal clearly that since the adoption of Structural Adjustment Programme (SAP), rate of growth of employment opportunities in the modern large scale sector (organized sector) has been declining steadily and has even become negative in recent years. Rate of growth of employment declined from 2.6% during 1980-81 to 0.4 %

during 1992-93, to (–) 0.3% in 1997-98 and further to (–) 0.6% in 2000-01 (Tata:

Statistical Abstracts 2003-04). The SAP also adversely affected both output and

employment of the conventional unorganized sector (Chakrabarty, 2002). Thus it is highly fallacious that indiscriminate establishment of large scale modern industries on the basis of unaltered foreign technology would generate additional employment (this is the essence of the slogan of the ruling party men in West Bengal). On the contrary, by both its direct and indirect impacts, it would make the unemployment situation more serious.

So the sustainable path of industrialization with employment generation, enhanced supply

of mass consumption goods, removal of poverty, preservation of environment, ecology and rural culture and on the whole well being of the majority, ought to be based on the

Gandhian concept of Swadeshi by revitalizing the craft sector, the history, prospects and

current problems of which are given below in brief.

Historical Background

A large number of highly efficient crafts flourished in ancient India as early as the 700 B.

C. the artisans in those days had acquired remarkable skill in all branches of crafts because of many conducive factors, which had emanated from ancient Indian tradition and socio economic conditions since the Vedic times (Buch, M. A. 1974, Vol.-I, pp. 116-236).

Kautilya, in his Arthaśāstra mentioned a large number of craft products (Kangle 1986, Chs. 11-13, 17, 18, 25, 33). These crafts were organized under strong guilds, which used to look after all relevant matters like supply of raw materials of appropriate specification and quality, inspection of quality and standard of products, arrangement of marketing facilities etc. (Panikkar, 1966, p. 36; Mookerjee 1980, pp. 601-602).

Till the early 19th century these crafts evinced great prosperity. East India Company's global trade depended considerably on craft products from India. The native kings and their courts used to generate considerable demand for high-quality and costly craft products.

However, these crafts faced a serious crisis since the mid 19th century because of inimical attitude of the British Rulers, degeneration of the kings and the noble class, and above all disintegration of the guilds by deliberate policies of British Administration. This resulted in decline of major crafts industries like cotton, woolen and silk textiles etc. (Gadgil 1973, Ch. 3, pp. 33-36). The plight of the artisans of innumerable other crafts was also precarious because of poverty, exploitation by middlemen and moneylenders, and erosion of market for high-quality costly craft products. Many artisans were compelled to leave their hereditary profession and seek employment elsewhere.

In recent decades there was a sign of revival of many crafts mainly through export (Economic Survey 2000-01, table-7.3 (A), pp. S-87, 88). But the existing problems coupled with the very recent craze for indiscriminate establishment of large scale industries in rural areas is likely to stultify this growth potential of these crafts unless the policies are reversed.

Employment Potential

The basic problem in analyzing employment potential of the craft industries in India is that it is very difficult to obtain reliable employment data as the crafts are widely scattered over the whole country. Employment data, as available from the 8th and 9th Five Year Plan documents, cover only a few industries like Khadi-cloth, handloom-cloth, raw silk, coir fiber etc. Total employment in these crafts increased from 18.43 million in 1984-85 to 32.83 million in 1996-97, the average annual rate of growth being 6.51 percent. This is remarkable considering the dismal performance of the organized sector in this regard.

In this connection it is worthwhile to have a brief glimpse of the performance of the

handloom sector vis-a- vis the mill sector in West Bengal. The remarkable performance of the handloom sector in West Bengal (where the slogan for unconditional development of large scale industries is most vociferous and even menacing to peace and security of

common people) presents an ironical picture. According to Government of West Bengal,

"Handloom industry is the largest cottage industry, which provides widest avenue for

employment opportunity. There are about 3,50,994 handlooms in the State providing full

time and part time employment to about 6,66,514 handloom weavers." (Economic Review, Govt. of W.B. 2004-05, p. 135). Production of handloom cloth in West Bengal increased from 401 million meters in 1995-96 to 1199.75 million meters in 2003-04 (Economic Review, Statistical Appendix, table 6.19, p. 127). In contrast cloth production in the mill sector was only 2.395 million meters (Ibid. table 6.3, p. 109).

From the above analysis it becomes clear that the crafts sector in India is expected to play a significant role in employment generation. But realization of this target is hardly possible if we do not adopt appropriate policies to resolve their existing problems, and on the contrary, choke the growth potential of these industries by our craze for large scale industries. The best way to revitalize these industries in line with the Gandhian concept of Swadeshi, is to organize the crafts under co-operatives modeled according to the ancient guilds, with the following tasks:

i) Maintenance of skill of the artisans and quality of the products.

ii) Arrangement of easy credit facilities for the artisans from banks and other financial institutions.

iii) Sales promotion in internal and foreign markets.

iv) Technology up gradation and re-designing.

v) Arrangement for collection of products from the small artisans, provision of storage

facilities and export promotion.

vi) Arrangements for supplying to the artisans raw materials of appropriate quality.

Formation of co-operatives with these tasks is the most worthwhile method for revival of

the numerous conventional and unconventional crafts in India so as to generate adequate

employment opportunities, enhance foreign exchange earning through them and initiate the practice of true Swadeshi to endow a human face to the process of globalization.

At the next step Swadeshi may be extended to small and ancillary sector catering to the

intermediate and accessories requirements of the large scale assembly sector. Taking a cue from Japan, most of the intermediates and accessories could be produced in small scale even in tiny sector without going through the hazards of large scale industries in all spheres.

Swadeshi does not preclude the import and assimilation of sophisticated foreign technology in case they are essential to keep this small sector technologically efficient and cost effective.

Notes

1. Young India: June 17, 1926.
2. Young India: May 12, 1927.
3, 4. 5. Speeches & Writings of M. Gandhi: P.385.
6, 7, 8. Mahatma: Vol. II, p. 53.
9. Mahatma: Vol. II, p. 53.
10. 11. Harijan: Nov. 30, 1934.
12. Harijan: Aug. 10, 1934
13. Mahatma: Vol. II, p. 53.
14, 15, 16, 17. Harijan: Dec. 7, 1934
18, 19. Harijan: Aug. 10, 1934
20, 21. Harijan: Nov. 30, 1934.
22, 23. Harijan: Mar 23, 1947
24, 25, 26. Young India: Oct. 13, 1921.
30, 31. Young India: May 13, 1919
32, 33. Young India: Mar. 7, 1929
34, 35, 36, 37. Constructive Programme: P.7.
38, 39. Young India: July 13, 1921
40. Young India: Dec. 8, 192141. Young India: May 12, 1927.
42, 43. Young India: Aug. 20, 1931
44, 45. Young India: July 13, 1921
46. Young India: May 15, 1924
47. Young India: Dec. 26, 1924.
48. Young India: June17, 1926
49, 50. Young India: July 1, 1926
51. Young India: June18, 1931
52. Young India: Aug. 20, 1931

References

Buch, M. A. (1979), *Economic Life in Ancient India*, R. S. Publishing House, Allahabad.

Gadgil, D. R. (1973), *Industrial Evolution in India in Recent Times*, Oxford University Press, Delhi.

Government of India, *Economic Survey*, 2000-01

Government of India, Planning Commission, *8th and 9th Five Year Plans.*

Government of West Bengal, *Economic Review* & *Statistical Abstract* 2004-05.

Kangle (1986), *Kautiliya Arthaśāstra* (English Translation), Motilal Banarasi Dass, Delhi.

M. K. Gandhi (1967), *The Gospel of Swadeshi*, Bhartiya Vidya Bhavan, Mumbai

Mookerji, R. K. (1980), "Economic Conditions" in Majumder (ed.), *The History and Culture of the Indian People*, Bharatiya Vidya Bhawan, Bombay.

Panikkar, K. M. (1966), *A Survey of Indian History*, Asia Publishing House, Bombay.

Sen, Abhijit (1996), "Economic Reforms, Employment and Poverty", *EPW*, Special Number.

Tata Services Limited: *Statistical Outline of India*, 2003-04.

Chapter 5. Laissez Faire and Crisis in Democracy in the New Millennium

Introduction

The new millennium, endorsing the paradigm of globalization, has been characterized by the revival of the concept of *laissez faire* conceived long ago by the French Physiocrats and later on corroborated by the neo-classicists. Karl Marx opposed this view and put forward his concept of socialism (as an interim path towards communism) based on a completely state-controlled centralized economic system. Later on, the mainstream *laissez faire* view was also challenged by Keynes and his followers who emphasized that State intervention is essential for sustainable development; but to this end, democracy instead of Marxian socialism is the better form of governance and there is no need to abandon the capitalistic mode of production. The newly independent countries after the Second World War, languishing in abject poverty and associated maladies, adopted various prescriptions of socialism and Keynesian economics and endeavoured to modernize their economies through excessive State intervention. The political set ups of these countries were both democratic and dictatorial.

However, during the late twentieth century both the socialist countries and the state-controlled mixed economies came up against serious economic crisis. By early 1990s

most of the socialist regimes crumbled and the mixed economies gradually started

adopting economic reforms based on LPG (Liberalization, Privatization and

Globalization). Thus once again there had been the revival of a *laissez faire* paradigm

through market-oriented reforms. But very few of the countries undertaking economic

reforms opted for a full-fledged free-market economy and State intervention in various

areas such as the social sector remained a common feature for most of these countries.

Prominent economists such as Amartya Sen and Joseph Stiglitz also suggested the

necessity of the state's role in these areas. In this context the question of the appropriate

political form to serve best this role arose. The most widely accepted view is that the

economics of a country is inexorably associated with the political set up and in this

regard historical experience shows that democracy is the most suitable form of polity for

the proper working of the *laissez faire* strategy with State intervention in specific areas.

But in most of the Least-Developed Countries (LDCs) like India, political corruption

based on the politician-criminal-police nexus has generated the most serious obstacle to

sustainable development.

This analysis aims at exploring the causes of such a predicament. The different segments of the article contain the following sub-topics: definition, origin and evolution of the concept of *laissez faire*; Adam Smith's approach; Marxian alternatives; neo-classical economic theories; the Keynesian alternative; collapse of Keynesianism and socialism; globalization, revival of *laissez faire* and its problems; the comparative efficacy of different forms of governance; the Smithian dilemma and the crisis of democracy

Laissez Faire

The exact origin of the French phrase *laissez faire* meaning "let do" or "permit to act" is uncertain and there are various folklores about its origin. The 18th century physiocrats, who popularized the phrase indicating economic liberalism and restriction on government intervention in economic activities, were not unanimous about its origin. Du Pont attributed it to Vincent de Gournay who was a strong advocate of deregulation of industry and removal of restrictions on trade in France. But the other physiocrats had different opinions. (see Higgs 2001, p.38). Later on the phrase was generally used to indicate a doctrine which maintains that private initiative and production should be free from economic interventionism and taxation by the State beyond the minimum requirement to maintain internal administration, security of private property and protection against foreign invasion. In this way the term became synonymous with 'free-market economy' and became a slogan of the economic libertarians.

According to these advocates of *laissez faire*, the free-market economy is superior to any controlled system to ensure sustainable development with equality, social justice and personal freedom. In such a system unrestricted market forces bring about desirable solutions to the basic economic problems, viz. what to produce, how to produce and for whom to produce.

Sometimes the term laissez faire became associated with the name of Adam Smith.

However, this interpretation has no valid basis. This confusion would be dispelled if we look more closely into the views of Adam Smith.

Adam Smith

Adam Smith, the 'father of modern economics', is mistakenly held by many as a proponent of *Laissez Faire*. This confusing idea has its root in partial study of the *Wealth of Nations* and above all ignorance about his earlier philosophical treatise *The Theory of Moral Sentiments*. In particular, his concept of the 'invisible hand' is mixed up with the concepts relevant to libertarianism.

The Smithian metaphor of the 'invisible hand', as used in *Wealth of Nations* and other writings of Smith, implies that in a free market economy if each individual maximizes his own revenue or satisfaction, then the total revenue and satisfaction of the society would be maximized, since the aggregate value for the society as a whole is the sum total of the individual values. An individual in isolation is, however, unaware of the aggregate result. Nor has he any power to directly influence the aggregate. So the mechanism of maximizing the aggregate value is not done by any individual by his own effort and intention. Thus it is conceived as being done by some 'invisible hand'.

Adam Smith categorically mentions the metaphor while asserting that any producer in a country will not employ his capital in foreign trade unless the profits available by thatmethod far exceed those available locally. This will also be beneficial for the society as a whole. In such a case the individual producer is guided by his self interest without any intention to serve the society, but the self-interest-based decision ultimately serves the society as a whole. Smith also argues in this context that by pursuing his own interest the economic agent frequently promotes that of the society more effectually than when he really intends to promote it. (Smith 1997, Vol. IV Chapter II.9, p.477)

Elsewhere Smith vividly explains how the pursuit of self-interest serves the interests of the society as a whole. To quote:

"It is not from the benevolence of the butcher, the brewer or the baker, that we expect our dinner, but from their regard to their own self interest. We address ourselves, not to their humanity but to their self-love, and never talk to them of our own necessities but of their advantages" (Smith 1776, Vol. I Chapter II.2, p.27).

According to many later economists the theory of the invisible hand implies that if each consumer is allowed to choose freely what to buy and each producer is allowed to choose freely what to sell and how to produce it, then the market will settle on a product

distribution and prices that are beneficial to the all individual members of a community,

and hence to the community as a whole. The reason for this is that greed will drive actors

to beneficial behavior. Efficient methods of production will be adopted in order to

maximize profits. Low prices will be charged in order to undercut competitors. Investors

will invest in those industries that are most urgently needed to maximize returns, and

withdraw capital from those that are less efficient in creating value.

Thus the concept of 'invisible hand' is at times mixed up with that of *Laissez Faire*. But a serious study of Smith would make it clear that he was by means an advocate of *Laissez Faire*. On the contrary, he opined for State interference in many cases. Smithian views regarding free market system and the capitalists are clear in the following excerpts:

The interest of the dealers, however, in any particular branch of trade or manufactures, is

always in some respects different from, and even opposite to, that of the public. To widen

the market and narrow the competition, is always the interest of the dealers. To widen the

market may frequently be agreeable enough to the interest of the public, but to narrow

the competition must always be against it, and can serve only to enable the dealers, by raising their profits above what they naturally would be, to levy, for their own benefit, an

absurd tax upon the rest of their fellow citizens.

"The proposal of any new law or regulation of commerce which comes from this order ought always to be listened to with great precaution, and ought never to be adopted till after having been long and carefully examined, not only with the most scrupulous, but

with the most suspicious attention. It comes from an order of men whose interest is never

exactly the same with that of the public, who have generally an interest to deceive and

even to oppress the public, and who accordingly have upon many occasions, both

deceived and oppressed it" (Smith 1776, Vol. I Chapter IX, p.207).

From the above quotation it is quite clear that Smith had no illusion that the spectacular material progress brought about by unrestrained activities of the capitalists would be an unmixed blessing for the human race as a whole. Apart from historical evidences, Smith put forward a theoretical justification too. On the basis of Smith's philosophical masterpiece, *The Theory of Moral Sentiments,* the basic sentiments of man can be broadly divided into two opposite categories: self-interest and fellow feeling. All the major sentiments belonging to either of these two categories are assumed by Smith to be endowed to man by nature. Thus,

"The great division of our affections is into the selfish and the benevolent" (Smith 1759, VII.II.4).

All human ethics belong to the second category of the Smithian sentiments, viz. 'fellow feeling', and they are likely to have a long history of evolution going down to the

association of the lower living beings (wolves, bees, ants etc.). Smith considers that material progress is brought about mainly by the motive of improving one's own

condition (a motive belonging to the self-interest category) and in its full manifestation it

becomes the dominant sentiment. Thus:

"It is this which first prompted them to cultivate the ground, to build houses, to found cities and commonwealths, and to invest and improve all the sciences and arts which ennoble and embellish human life, which have entirely changed the whole face of the globe, have turned the rude forests of nature into agreeable and fertile plains, and made the trackless and barren ocean a new fund of subsistence and the great high road of communication to the different nations of the earth" (Ibid. IV.I.10).

However, it "....is the cause of all the tumult and bustle, all the rapine and injustice which avarice and ambition have introduced into this world" (Ibid. I.III.23).

The capitalistic system opens up vast possibilities of betterment of the conditions of the traders and industrialists and in their reckless drive towards achieving higher and higher material gains, all ethical sentiments, fellow feeling and human values are bound to be swept away unless restrained by some outside force.

As regards this outside force, Smith argues that all our notions of moral and ethical

senses which as such are helpless in a conflict with self interest may be made effective by

converting them into positive laws. The important steps in this regard as described by

Smith are:

"It is thus the general rules of morality are formed. They are ultimately founded upon

experience of what, in particular instances, our moral faculties, our normal sense of merit and propriety, approve or disapprove of. We do not originally approve or condemn particular actions because, upon examination, they appear to be agreeable or consistent with a general rule. The general rule, on the contrary, is formed by finding, from experience that all actions of a certain kind, or circumstanced in a certain manner, are approved or disapproved of" (Ibid. III.I.95).

The general rules of morality can be effective only if they are framed into positive laws of justice:

"As the violation of justice is what men will never submit to from one another, the public magistrate is under the necessity of employing the power of the commonwealth to enforce the practice of this virtue" (Ibid. VII.IV.36).

These laws of justice can be framed also to restrain the harmful activities of the 'dealers' (the Smithian term meaning the capitalists and merchants). Smith was by no means an advocate of the '*laissez faire*' doctrine and he, in fact, was in favor of imposing State regulations on the 'class' whose interest, he unequivocally considered, was always opposite to that of the public. This is an effort, though in embryonic form, towards devising an alternative to the free market capitalism. But here he is confronted with an insurmountable obstacle which we shall take up once again at the concluding section of this article.

Marxian Approach

Marxian theories of the historical process of development of the human society provide strong accounts of the genesis of poverty and inequality. From the economic standpoint,

Marx divides the process of development of human society till his time into four major

stages: primitive communism, slave society, feudalism and capitalism. He predicts that

capitalism would be replaced by socialism, which again will ultimately dissolve into the

stage of communism. Marxian process of evolution of human society is being elaborated

in various writings of both Karl Marx and his friend and adherent Frederick Engels:

At the first stage, during primitive communism, poverty in the modern sense did not exist

(poverty in the modern sense is meaningful only when its opposite, viz. opulence, exists).

It was simply limitation of amenities, applicable to all members of a clan, because of

limited knowledge to explore natural resources to meet human demand. These clan

societies were characterized by equality. Whatever necessities they gathered through

their limited command over Nature, were divided among members according to the

requirement of each (Engels 1884, Ch-IX, p.155). Furthermore:

Man-nature conflict gradually led to improvement in methods of production – man

gradually having more and more command over Nature with its increasing knowledge.

With acceleration of this process by increasing social division of labour, surplus over and

above consumption requirements started emerging. And at the same time human values pertaining to fellow feeling and equality started degenerating into slavery – oppression of one class of people by another (Ibid. pp. 157-160).

Engels explains how with the emergence of money as the most convenient medium of exchange and the emergence of the parasitic merchant class, the process of property ownership and accumulation of wealth by a few and the consequent poverty and inequality were further crystallized (Ibid. pp.162-163). This process was then further intensified:

Continued material progress, made possible by increasing command over Nature, ultimately paved the way for the Industrial Revolution, which ushered in the capitalistic or bourgeois society. Capitalism enhanced the pace of materialistic development but at the same time it generated more ruthless exploitation of the labour class turning them into proletariats and mere commodities to be sold to the bourgeoisie, i.e. the capitalists (Marx and Engels 1848, Ch-1, p. 51).

According to Marx and Engels the basic causes of oppression, exploitation, and increasing poverty and inequality along with material progress were the class society and the institution of private property with the associated vices such as the division of labour, exchange, family structure, competition and the institution of the State. Let us have a brief glimpse of the Marxian view regarding these factors.

Private Property

According to the Marxian world outlook, private property is the basic cause of all maladies in human society. So the task of the communists is to abolish all private property, which is both cause and consequence of 'alienated' or 'estranged' labor. Division of labor, competition, exchange, family and all other corrupting

elements of society, have originated from private property and estranged labour (Marx

1974, pp. 61-74). Thus, Marx and Engels assert that the first and foremost task of the

communists opting for a society free from exploitation, poverty, inequality and injustice

is to abolish the institution of private property, held so sacred by the non-Marxists (Marx

and Engels 1848, p. 63).

Division of Labor and Exchange

Just like private property, the division of labour is considered by Marx and Engels as another evil responsible for all the maladies in human society. Division of labour, according to them, has undermined the collective nature of production, given rise to exchange between individuals and thereby facilitated the process of appropriation of surplus value and economic exploitation. It is nothing but the expression of estranged, alienated positing of human activity. It increases immensely the wealth and refinement of society indeed, but at the same time impoverishes the worker and turns him into a machine (Marx 1974, pp. 26-27, 113; Engels 1884, p.171). Abolition of division of labour, Engels assures, would create no problem at all as appropriate education would enable young people to quickly familiarize themselves with the whole system of production and to pass from one branch of production to another in response to the needs of society or their own inclinations (Engels 1969, pp.93- 94).

Family

Marx considers family to be another serious evil generated from private property relations and evolved through various stages of economic advancement. The origin of family was necessitated by the emergence of agricultural production in the pre-capitalist production relations. With the emergence of capitalistic system the basic necessity for the institution of family being weakened, the family system started degenerating. In the bourgeois society, according to Marx and Engels, although family is still held as a sacred institution, bourgeois family has in reality turned into an instrument of suppression and exploitation of women by men and has degeneration in adultery and prostitution. They opine that among the proletariat, on the other hand, the family in the bourgeois sense is virtually non existent. So, in a communist society, the family would no longer exist as the basis of its existence, viz. private property, would be non-existent (Marx and Engels 1848, pp. 68-70).

Engels further emphasizes that abolition of private property would remove the two bases of traditional marriage and family, viz. dependence of women on men and that of children on the parents. And so marriage and family would perish, transforming the relations between the sexes into a purely private matter free from any intervention by the society or the State (Engels 1969, p.94).

Competition

According to Marxian view, competition, another consequence of private property, has been the propelling force as well as the cause of disorder of bourgeois society. In this connection Marx contradicts the commonly held view that monopoly is opposed to competition and opines that competition and monopoly are but two sides of the same coin. (Marx 1974, p.177 [Appendix]) Competition has, however, its positive side also as it creates condition under which the capitalistic system collapses (Marx 1966, pp. 130-31). The task of the communists is to accentuate this process. This is to be donethrough abolition of private property and establishment of the communal ownership of goods (Engels 1969, p. 89).

The State

According to Marxian view, the Sate is an institution developed solely to protect the interests of the exploiter minority against that of the exploited majority and to facilitate the process of exploitation (Engels 1884, pp.166-169). So at a certain stage of development of productive forces, when the existence of class division would be not only unnecessary but also a positive hindrance to further advancement of productive forces, classes and along with them the State would disappear, preserved only in the museum of antiquities (Ibid. p.170).

Transition

Although human society, according to Marx, would automatically bring about communism by the inherent contradictions, but it may take a very long time. So he suggests that this process of transition towards the ultimate goal is to be hastened by means of deliberate effort. Capitalism has already generated the force, viz. the proletariats, which can play a crucial role in accelerating this pace by overthrowing the bourgeois Sate and establish the socialist State under the dictatorship of the proletariat and thereby pave the path towards communism. The weapon of the proletariat is the same 'class struggle' which has been the driving force of human history ever since the emergence of private property.

Class Struggle

According to the Marxist view, the driving force of human civilization has been the class struggle, the relentless war between the exploiters and the exploited (Marx and Engels 1848, p. 40). This class antagonism, during the capitalist system, has been reduced to the struggle between two distinct classes (Ibid. p. 41). With the expansion of capitalistic production the size and strength of the proletariat working class is continuously increasing and thus from within the capitalistic system a force is born that will ultimately overthrow this system (Ibid. pp. 50-51). So the first step is to organize the proletariats under the communist party and inspire them to overthrow the bourgeois State and replace it with the socialist State under the dictatorship of the proletariat (Engels 1975, pp. 326-27).

Unfortunately, Marx and Engels failed to realize (because of either superficial observation or myopic view or parochial attachments) that causes of poverty, inequality, exploitation and similar maladies do not lie in private property, family relations, the state or any other visible phenomenon, but it lies deep in human nature, in unethical elements such as greed, pride, jealousy and so on. Thus, eradication of the maladies, if at all possible, needs to be accomplished by some process that would reduce the prevalence of these basic vices in human mind. Occasionally, however, they have touched upon the real causes of the maladies such as greed, jealousy, etc. (Marx 1974, pp. 62, 88; Engels 1884, p. 173). But these fleeting moments of digression to reality soon dissolved into the preaching of their invented doctrine. The Marxist weapon to overthrow the bourgeois State is the proletariat class, the labour class forced down to the level of bare subsistence (Marx 1974, p. 61).

It cannot be denied that such a proletariat class had real existence in all the nascent capitalist countries during the time of Marx (the nineteenth century). But with technological advancement during the twentieth century, the scenario changed radically. The proletarian class, 'who had nothing to lose but chains', in the capitalist countries, gradually diminished in size in course of technological progress during the twentieth century and almost vanished with the onset of the new millennium. The relatively better paid labourers of the modern capitalist countries could hardly be inspired to raise arms against the capitalists, unlike their proletariat brethren a century ago. Moreover, class composition in the modern capitalist countries has become extremely complex with the swelling of various grades of the middle class. This has belied the Marxian conviction that under capitalism the society would be polarized into two distinct classes: capitalists and labourers.

Unfortunately, because of their myopic vision and pre-occupation with invented doctrine, Marx and Engels failed to visualize the future world that capitalism would usher in. So, ultimately, in the real world, Marxism degenerated into Leninism and Maoism, aiming at overthrowing the State by organizing the poverty stricken masses of the feudal and semi-feudal countries. Marx and Engels, however, had dubbed this sort of endeavour as utopian socialism (Engels 1975 pp. 293, 3003).

Ultimate Goal

The ultimate goal of Marxist process is to achieve communism. But the transition from socialism to communism would be a long historical process. Under communism, there would be no private property, no family, no State, no competition, no division of labour, and no exchange (Marx 1974, p. 91). Even most of the radical Marxists today consider this as sheer utopia.

The Neo-classical Approach

Neoclassical economics, a common name for a wide variety of ideas, is conventionally ascribed to William Stanley Jevons (1871), Carl Menger (1871) and Leon Walras (1877) although roots of the theory may be traced in the writings of John Stuart Mill (1848).

Later on Alfred Marshall (1890, pp. 269-278) added a new dimension to neo-classical economics by clearly pointing out that both demand and supply, like the two blades of a scissors, play equally important role in determining prices. He explained prices by the intersection of supply and demand curves. In the 20th century, economists such as J. R. Hicks, Joan Robinson, Camberlin, and Paul Samuelson made important contributions to this stream of economic thought and added statistical and mathematical sophistication to treatment of economic concepts.

The three basic premises of neo-classical economics[1] are:

1. Both consumers and producers are rational.

2. Consumers maximize utility and firms maximize profits.

3. People act independently on the basis of full and relevant information.

On the basis of the above basic assumptions, neoclassical economists built a structure to understand the allocation of scarce resources among alternative ends. The basic tasks of an economy (viz. what to produce, how to produce and for whom to produce) are all determined in the market by the interaction of demand and supply without any government intervention.

The neo-classical economists held that at the micro level demand and supply of both final commodities and factors of production are determined through the maximization of satisfaction of the consumer and that of profit of the firm. The type and level of output to be produced (what to produce) and, the input-mix and the technology to be used (how to produce) are all determined by the interplay of demand and supply in the market without any outside intervention. 'For whom to be produced' is also determined in the market on the basis of demand and purchasing power, which is again determined in the factor market.

The neo-classical economists laid most emphasis on micro behaviour of the economic agents as they held that all macro level results could be determined by aggregating micro values.

In brief, neo-classical economics emphasized that for rational allocation and perfect functioning of the economy, a free-market mechanism without government intervention is the best, and thus laid support to the *laissez faire* doctrine. This school of thought dominated mainstream economics till the early 1930s. But the 'great depression' of the 1930s shattered all complacency with the neo-classical economics and resulted in the emergence of Keynesian economics.

The Keynesian Approach

The great depression of the 1930s dealt a heavy blow to neo-classical assertion that all economic problems could be solved through the free-play of the market forces of demand and supply and State intervention in economic activities is unnecessary. In this backdrop, the J. M. Keynes drew the attention of the world by publishing his great treatise: *General Theory on Employment, Interest and Money* (1936) in which he put forward a solution to the anomalies of free market capitalism without any Marxian authoritarian system but advocating State intervention, mainly through fiscal policy within a democratic political system. Thus he appeared as the savior of capitalism from the crisis predicted by Karl Marx (Hansen 1953).

In brief, Keynesian economics advocates a mixed economy, in which both the State and the private sector are considered to play an important role. Thus Keynesian approach markedly differs from both *laissez-faire* economic liberalism, which advocates that markets and the private sector operate best without State intervention, and a Marxian approach calling for a centrally controlled economy with no virtual role of the private sector.

Keynes also asserted that aggregate results may not be just the sum total of individual outcomes and therefore micro-economic solutions may not be reflected at the macro level. Here the Keynesian approach radically differs from the micro-based neoclassical approach. Keynes emphasized a general theory in which utilization of resources could be high or low, whereas neoclassical economists highlighted the particular case of full utilization.

Contradicting the classical and neoclassical emphasis on production and supply, Keynes laid primary emphasis on aggregate demand for goods as the driving force of the economy. From this he argued that government fiscal policies could be used to promote demand at a macro level, to obviate unemployment and deflation as evident during the 1930s. Keynes argued that the government can play a crucial role to stimulate the economy during depression through the combination of reduction of interest rates, tax cuts and enhancement of autonomous investment, especially in infrastructure. Thus, unlike the classical and neoclassical economists, Keynes advocated a deficit budget instead of a balanced or surplus budget during depression.

Keynes vehemently opposed the classical view that there is a strong automatic tendency for output and employment to move toward full employment levels. He argued that because of wage-price inflexibility, once the economy is away from full employment situation, it would not return to full employment automatically and an underemployment equilibrium would be the outcome. Only government intervention, he held, could restore full-employment.

After Keynes, Keynesian analysis was combined with neoclassical economics. This combination, known as 'the neoclassical synthesis', dominated mainstream macroeconomic thought till the seventies of the last century (see Goodfriend & King 1998; Mankiw & Romer 1991). In the post-war years Keynesian ideas were widely accepted by many governments as guidelines for framing economic policies. To this end the Hicksian IS-LM model served as the practical guideline for determining actual economic policies (Hicks 1937; IS represents 'Investment and Saving equilibrium' while LM refers to 'Liquidity preference and Money supply equilibrium'). The IS-LM model relates aggregate demand and employment to three exogenous quantities, i.e., the amount of money in circulation, the government budget, and the state of business expectations (Branson 1979, Chapters 4-6).

Another important tool for framing Keynesian policy was the Phillips Curve, which depicted an inverse relation between employment and inflation. By using this mechanism a government can decide which combination of unemployment and inflation would be suitable for the economy concerned (Ibid. Chapter 18).

The Collapse of Keynesian Era and Socialist Regimes

Post-war years till the early 1970s saw the upswing of Keynesian economics. But the situation was reversed after the oil shock of 1973. During this period a combination of high inflation and high unemployment (stagflation), contradicting the Phillips Curve concept, called for simultaneous expansionary and contractionary policies if a Keynesian solution was sought, but this was absurd.[2] This dilemma led to the emergence of monetarism, supply-side economics and new classical economics all indicating a reversal of the Keynesian approach and advocating return of the mixed economies to a more market oriented system.[3] All these ushered in the era of liberalization and structural reforms of the mixed economies. In the mean time most of the socialist economies, including their leader the USSR, collapsed and all of them opted for the capitalistic path (Basu, 1999).

Within a decade or so many countries introduced economic reforms and some of them, including the so-called 'East Asian Tigers', achieved spectacular success after liberalization. This encouraged many other countries such as India to pursue economic liberalization. In the meantime the communication revolution hastened the process of globalization based on liberalization of foreign trade, which was crystallized with the emergence of the World Trade Organization (WTO).

Globalization and It's Hazards

The era of globalization emerged during the 1980s and with the gradual liberalization of most of the socialist and mixed economies it assumed full-fledged form during the 1990s.

The spectacular communication revolution, which turned the world almost into a global village, facilitated the process considerably. Along with the Structural Reforms insisted on by the IMF (International Monetary Fund) and the World Bank, the newly established

WTO completed the process through its policy of free-trade for all the member countries.

In the new era there was a paradigm shift from State control to a market orientation. Thus

there had been a revival of the *laissez faire* regime. However, with the passage of time,

the new era started revealing very many hazards associated with this process, such as

increased unemployment, market failures and increasing inter-nation and intra-nation

disparities.

With this backdrop, economists such as Amartya Sen (Dreze & Sen 1989) and Joseph Stiglitz started strongly emphasizing the importance of State intervention in specific areas (Stiglitz 2002 & 2006; Stiglitz *et. al* 2006). Their views received wide acceptance but the question arose as to which form of governance would be most suitable for this purpose. In this context we may briefly undertake a brief comparison of the efficacy of various

forms of government.

Comparative Efficacy of Different Forms of Governance

Dictatorship: Historical experience of all forms of non-socialist dictatorial regimes (in

the past and the present) has revealed their overwhelmingly oppressive features.[4] So we rule out this form as unsuitable.

Monarchy: Ancient Indian Texts (especially Manusmriti and Arthaśāstra of Kautilya)[5]

have laid down detailed rules and procedures to make an ideal king (Basu 2005).

Unfortunately, in recorded history, except for Aśoka (Thapar 1961; Sastri 1967, pp.201-

48; Kosambi 1981, pp.157-65), there is no evidence of the existence of another ideal king. The great Greek philosopher Plato conceived of a philosopher king (Plato 1901, pp.215-40) as an ideal pattern of government. However, his concept of a 'philosopher king' was attacked as during the European enlightenment. Immanuel Kant made the interesting comment: "That 'kings will philosophize or philosophers become kings,' is not to be expected. Nor indeed is it to be desired, because the possession of power inevitably corrupts the free judgment of reason." (Kant 1795). Plato later on abandoned this idea after a bitter experience in attempting to reform the ruler of Syracuse.[6] So monarchy is ruled out.

Socialism: Like the Indian concept of Ideal King or Plato's philosopher king, socialism is also a utopian concept. It differs in one respect, viz. unlike the former two concepts the means to achieve its goal is the violent 'class struggle'. Such a class struggle cannot be the solid basis for an enduring state system or a productive economy. This is the basic reason that compelled the USSR, the first and the most powerful socialist state, to revert back to capitalistic path in the early 1990s. (Basu 1999)

Democracy: Now we are left with democracy, which, from the standpoint of human freedom, is the best conceivable form of government. Amartya Sen has emphasized the role of public opinion and the mass media in ensuring proper functioning of democracy.

(Dreze & Sen 1989, pp. 278-79). However, the present state of democracy in the world

and associated global trends are not at all encouraging. Sen's hopes, placed on the masses

and the media to make democracy really meaningful, come up against the Smithian

dilemma.

The Smithian Dilemma and the Crisis of Democracy

Adam Smith unequivocally explained why material achievements in the form of

economic power are conceived as the best server of self-interest of an individual in spite

of all personal hazards associated with it. Here Smith goes deep into basic human

psychology and puts forward his findings from empirical observations. An inherent

nature of any human being, whatever his own position, is to praise and worship

successful and rich people, however immoral be the means by which this opulence has

been achieved. Moreover, most people nurture in their subconscious the hidden desire toachieve opulence and fame so as to get the praise and approbation of all and sundry.

(Smith 1759, I.III.28-31)

This basic nature of the masses belies all hopes to bring corrupt politicians to the path of ethics and virtue. The inner discipline of all the major political parties makes it

impossible for the ordinary members to protest against the mischief of the leaders.

Moreover 'leader worship' because of this Smithian psychosis impels the cadres, members and supporters of political parties to ignore the heinous activities of the leaders.

The corrupt politicians also inculcate the inherent corrupt mentality of the common people. Thus the politicians get absolute freedom to do whatever best serves their personal interest even at the cost of the society and the masses. This belies all our hopes to eradicate poverty and social injustice through the democratic system, the last conceivable place of hope.

We once again come back to the Marxian conviction that deprivation, injustice and exploitation cannot be eradicated so long as private property and along with it the division of labour, competition, exchange, family structures and the State remain in existence. In brief, classless communism is the only real solution. Now if we consider Marxian communism a pure utopia, we are relegated to a hopeless dilemma as none has yet been able to devise an alternative.

Notes

1. For an analysis of neo-classical economics and its various aspects see [http://williamking.www.drexel.edu/top/Prin/txt/Neoch/Eco111s1.html].

2. For one account see [http://en.wikipedia.org/wiki/Stagflation#Early_Keynesianism_and_monetarism_and_the_Phillips_curve].

3. For detail see [http://pages.stern.nyu.edu/~nroubini/SUPPLY.HTM] [http://en.wikipedia.org/wiki/Supplyside_economics].

4. See Black 1986 and Fitch and Lowenthal (eds.) 1986 for the heinous roles of dictatorial regimes in Latin America. Amitav Ghosh's novel "The Glass Palace" (Ghosh 2001) portrays a vivid account of the oppressive dictatorial regime in Myanmar (Burma).

5. See Manusmriti: chapter-7, ślokas: 30-49, 58, 79, 142-47, 221-26 (*Sacred Books of the East*, Vol. XXV, edited by F. Max Muller, Oxford Clarendon Press, 1888) and Arthaśāstra of Kautilya: book-I: ch-5/7-17; ch-6/1-10; ch-7/1-8; ch-9/6-25; ch-19/9-11 (Kangle 1986).

6 According to the Greek author Diogenes Laertius, Plato received an invitation from Dionysius, the king of Syracuse to turn his kingdom into utopia and Plato readily accepted the invitation. But when Plato suggested the king either to become a philosopher himself or to relinquish power for some philosopher in order to make his kingdom a utopia, the king became infuriated with Plato and sold him as a slave.

Fortunately Plato's disciple Anniceris appeared in time as a rescuer by repurchasing Plato from the slave trader. These events disillusioned Plato. (For this account see Laertius 2001, book-3, XIV-XVIII).

References

Basu, Ratan Lal (1999): "Material Progress and Ethics: a Pilgrimage Through Time" in *The Culture Mandala* (The Bulletin of the Center for East-West Cultural and Economic Studies, Bond University, Australia), Vol.4, No.1, December 1999-January 2000. [http://www.international-relations.com].

Basu, Ratan Lal (2005): "Human Development Part 2: Ancient Kingship, Modern Politicians and the Problem of Corruption in India" in *The Culture Mandala*, Vol.7, No.1, December [http://www.international-relations.com].

Black, Jan Knippers (1986): *Sentinels of Empire: The United States and Latin American Militarism*, Greenwood Press, New York.

Branson, William H. (1979): *Macroeconomic Theory and Policy*, Harper & Row, New York.

Dreze, Jean and Sen, Amartya (1989): *Hunger and Public Action*, Oxford India Paperbacks, New Delhi, 1999.

Engels, Frederick (1969): "The Principles of Communism", *Marx-Engels Selected Works*, Volume-I, p. 81-97, Progress Publishers, Moscow.

Engels, Frederick (1975): *Anti-Dühring*, Progress Publishers, Moscow.

Engels, Frederick (1884): *The Origin of the Family, Private Property and the State*, Progress Publishers, Moscow, 1972.

Fitch, J. Samuel and Abraham F. Lowenthal (eds.) (1986): *Armies and Politics in Latin America*, Holmes & Meier, New York.

Ghosh, Amitav (2001): *The Glass Palace*, HarperCollins, New York.

Goodfriend, Marvin & King, Robert G. (1998), "the New Neoclassical Synthesis and the Role of Monetary Policy", *Working Paper 98-05*, Federal Reserve Bank of Richmond [http://ideas.repec.org/p/fip/fedrwp/98-05.html]

Hansen, Alvin H. (1953): *A Guide to Keynes*, McGraw-Hill, New York.

Hicks, J. R. (1937), "Mr. Keynes and the Classics", *Econometrica*, April.

Higgs, Henry (2001): *The Physiocrats*, Batoche Books, Kitchener.

Jevons, William Stanley (1871), *Theory of Political Economy*, Macmillan & Co., Third Edition, London, 1888.

Kangle, R. P. (1986), *Kautīliya Arthaśāstra*, Part-II [English translation], Motilal Banarasidass, Delhi.

Kant, Immanuel (1795): "Perpetual Peace", in *Kant's Principles of Politics,including his essay on Perpetual Peace, A Contribution to Political Science,* trans. W. Hastie, Clark, Edinburgh, 1891.

Keynes, John Maynard, (1936), *The General Theory of Employment, Interest and Money*, Marxist Org. 2002 [http://www.marxists.org/reference/subject/economics/keynes/general-theory]

Kosambi, D.D. (1981): *The Culture and Civilization of Ancient India*, Vikas Publishing House, New Delhi.

Laertius, Diogenes (2001): *Lives of Eminent Philosophers*, Vol. I, translated by R.D.Hicks, Harvard University Press.

Mankiw, N. Gregory & Romer, David (eds.), (1991), *New Keynesian Economics*, MIT Press.

Marshall, Alfred (1890): *Principles of Economics*, Macmillan & C0. Ltd., London, Eighth edition, 1961.

Marx and Engels (1848): *Manifesto of the Communist Party*, Progress Publishers, Moscow, 1975.

Marx, Karl (1966): *The Poverty of Philosophy*, Progress Publishers, Moscow.

Marx, Karl (1974): *Economic and Philosophic Manuscript of 1848*, Progress Publishers, Moscow.

Max Muller, F. (ed.) (1888): *Sacred Books of the East*, Vol. XXV, Oxford Clarendon Press.

Menger, Carl (1871): *Principles of Economics*, Ludvwig Von Mises Institute, Alabama, 2007.

Mill, John Stuart (1848): *Principles of Political Economy*, Prometheus Books (Great Minds Series), New York, 2004.

Muller, F. Max (ed.) (1888) *Sacred Books of the East*, Vol. XXV, Oxford Clarendon Press, 1888.

Plato (1901): *The Republic*, edited and translated by Benjamin Jowett, P. F. Collier & Son, New York.

Sastri, K.A.Nilakanta (ed.) (1967); *Age of the Nandas and Mauryas*, Motilal Banarasidass, Delhi.

Sen, Amartya (1970): *Collective Choice and Social Welfare*, North-Holland, Amsterdam, 1979.

Smith, Adam (1759): *The Theory of Moral Sentiments*, A. Millar, Sixth edition, London, 1790.

Smith, Adam (1776): *An Inquiry into the Nature and Causes of the Wealth of Nations*, Vol. 4, the 1776 Glasgow & the 1776 University of Chicago Edition.

[http://www.ibiblio.org/ml/libri/s/SmithA_WealthNations_p.pdf].

Stiglitz, Joseph, E. (2002): *Globalization and Its Discontents*, W.W. Norton & Company.

Stiglitz, Joseph, E. (2006): *Making Globalization Work*, Penguin Books.

Stiglitz, Joseph, E. et. al. (2006): *Stability with Growth: Macroeconomics, Liberalization, and Development*, Initiative for Policy Dialogue Series C, Oxford University Press.

Thapar, Romila (1961): *Asoka and the Decline of the Mauryas*, Oxford University Press, New Delhi.

Walras, Leon (1877): *Elements of Pure Economics*, Harvard University Press, 1954.

Chapter 6. Cauvery Eggs and Salesman's Social Choice

Anyone who has happened to pass through the galleries of the Cauvery Emporium at Bangalore city must have been marveled by the variegated articles and exquisite sandalwood images displayed therein. At the end of December 1998, while strolling leisurely along the M. G. Road in an endeavour to escape the oppression of economic theories (showering mercilessly in the proceedings of the Annual Conference of the Indian Economic Association), I suddenly, as though goaded by whim, decided to have a shopping venture through the Cauvery Emporium. In course of an hour long journey through the Cauvery World, multitudes of articles enticed me, but my purchase ultimately ended up with a dozen multicolored wooden eggs.

Why only the wooden eggs?

First, because the other choice worthy articles displayed there and having higher utility to me than the wooden eggs were beyond the purchasing capability permitted by the money in my purse.

Second, because the other more desirable things affordable by my purse could not be found in the Emporium. So, it comes out that consumer's choice (on which the modern economists attach much significance) is conditioned by:

i) Money in the consumer's purse and

ii) Things offered for sale by the vendor.

Let us have a deeper look into the situation. I desired to purchase things (preferable to the wooden eggs) affordable by my purse. But they were not there in the Emporium. So we see that besides money affordable by the buyer, consumer's choice is delimited by the things produced and offered for sale by the sellers. The pertinent question is: has consumer's choice any role in influencing the production and sales decisions of the firms? It is not so if the sellers have the power to make the consumers buy whatever they offer for sale and certainly they would offer things which fetch highest profit and not ones giving maximum utility and satisfaction to the buyer. They should only master the methods to mould consumer's choices in their own way.

Before stepping into the Emporium I hardly had any idea about the wooden eggs. I came upon them for the first time and among the affordable articles there they seemed to be the best as gifts. In a way this was a forced choice considering the fact that I had no time to try other shops. All such forced choices are not, however, generated at first sight, but persistent sales efforts can accomplish it in course of time.

Let us consider an extreme case. Smokers and tobacco chewers have fascination for nicotine, a deadly alkaloid if taken in poisonous doses. They are not fatal in infinitesimal doses as in cigarettes, *zerdas* etc. but accumulation leads to slow poisoning and various serious ailments. To the un-addicted, tobacco is repulsive and nauseating. But demonstration effect may encourage one to try it and in course of time his neuron code gets distorted generating a feeling of liking and attraction for the pernicious substance. According to drug experts this distortion is very rapid and deep seated if one tries the opium derived alkaloid 'heroine'.

In fact, consumer's choice is vulnerable to demonstration effect, which could be generated through repeated advertising. With the knowledge of mass psychology, the sellers can mould the choice pattern of the consumers so as to facilitate sales of commodities most beneficial to them whatever the impact on the consumers. Strong consumer choices, if any, for unprofitable wares, could be nipped in the bud simply by not producing them.

The objective of the sellers is either to maximize profit or to maximize sales and capture new markets (either by out competing rivals or by attracting new buyers). Sales efforts through advertising, replacement of old commodities by new ones etc. are adopted to achieve these goals. Aggressive sales efforts, in fact, make the consumer irrational and flummoxed. He fails to distinguish on his own between good and bad commodities, necessary and unnecessary commodities, and cannot judge for himself what is beneficial or harmful for him. In a sense being swept by the flood of advertising he virtually loses his own identity and floats aimlessly like a dead leaf being surrendered to the designs of the advertisers. Aggressing advertising and psychological warfare, against the pattern of choice of the consumers not conducive to the profit or sales of the firms, demolish all the basic premises of theories of social choice based on consumer's sovereignty. Being hypnotized by advertising, consumers turn into mere playthings at the hands of the sellers.

Thus social choice virtually turns out to be Salesman's Social Choice.

But here the salesmen are likely to come up against a serious backfire. In the Cauvery Episode, we have seen that demand by a consumer depends not only on goods available and advertised of, but also on the money affordable by him which is ultimately dependent on the income of the consumer. Thus the profit/sales maximizing efforts of the multinational corporations (MNCs) are likely to bring about a pattern of income distribution, which would strike back '*a la boomerang*'. Lack of adequate income of the majority of consumers (a direct consequence of the sales maximizing efforts of the MNCs) may constrain the efforts of the MNCs to enhance the global aggregate sales proceeds. Here lies the inner contradiction and self-defeating aspect of the global economic situation dominated by the MNCs and where global welfare means welfare of the sales men, especially the giant MNCs.

Recent Global Economic Crisis is simply a natural outcome of the production process dictated by Salesman's Social Choice and not any Special Situation.

About the Author

The author of this volume Dr. Ratan Lal Basu is a Ph. D. in Economics (on Arthaśāstra, the treatise on political economy and statecraft composed by a Brāhmaṇa scholar Kauṭilya around 300 B. C.). He retired as principal from a Government-Sponsored College at Kolkata, and after retirement got fully occupied with research and publishing activities pertaining to Indology, ancient economics, modern economic problems, economic history, yoga and tantra cult, statecraft, international relations and espionage, ethics and morality and also fiction in English and Bengali (his mother tongue).

www.ingramcontent.com/pod-product-compliance
Lightning Source LLC
LaVergne TN
LVHW091114150826
845673LV00002B/817

* 9 7 9 8 2 1 5 5 1 3 6 3 7 *